Creative Writing: the Matrix

Exercises & Ideas for Creative Writing Teachers

Susan Lee Kerr

Paxton
⌘

For Michael, who grew me.

The author gratefully acknowledges permission to reprint or adapt from the following works: From *Fiction Writer's Workshop* copyright © 1998 by Josip Novakovich. Used with the kind permission of Betterway Books, a division of F+W Publications, Inc., Cincinnati, Ohio. All rights reserved. From *Five-minute Activities: A Resource Book of Short Activities* by Penny Ur and Andrew Wright, Cambridge University Press, Cambridge, 1992. From *Get Writing* website, www.bbc.co.uk/dna/getwriting/ British Broadcasting Company, London. From *The Time of Your Life* by Sheila Dainow, Boxtree, PanMacmillan, London, 1994. From *The Weekend Novelist* by Robert J Ray, Dell, New York, 1994. From *Writing Down the Bones,* by Natalie Goldberg, © 1986. Reprinted by arrangement with Shambhala Publications, Inc., Boston, www.shambhala.com Excerpt from pages 103-4, totalling 86 words from *Writing for Your Life* by Deena Metzger, copyright © 1992 by Deena Metzger. Reprinted by permission of HarperCollins Publishers. From *Writing on Both Sides of the Brain,* by Henriette Anne Klauser, HarperCollins, San Francisco, © 1986. Reprinted with kind permission of the author, www.henrietteklauser.com
All rights reserved.

The author also acknowledges and thanks the following authors, poets and tutors who have given permission to include their exercises, ideas or text and have personally well-wished this book: Gillian Allnutt, Kate Clanchy, Sheila Dainow, Henriette Anne Klauser, Robert J Ray, Susan Sellers, Barbara Trapido.

Every effort has been made to trace copyright for material in the book not listed above. The author and publisher would be happy to make arrangements with any holder of copyright whom it has not been possible to trace by the time of going to press.

Creative Writing: the Matrix, Exercises & Ideas for Creative Writing Teachers.
Copyright © 2007 by Susan Lee Kerr.
First published 2007 by Paxton Publishing, 55 Burlington Lane, London W4 3ET

The right of Susan Lee Kerr to be identified as the author of this work has been asserted by her in accordance with the Copyright, Designs and Patents Act 1988.

All rights reserved. No part of this publication may be reproduced, stored in or introduced into a retrieval system, or transmitted, in any form, or by any means (electronic, mechanical, photocopying, recording or otherwise) without the prior written permission of the publisher. Any person who does any unauthorized act in relation to this publication may be liable to criminal prosecution and civil claims for damages.

British Library Cataloguing in Publication Data. A catalogue record for this book is available from the British Library.

Typeset by West 4 Printers, London
Printed and bound in Great Britain by
Biddles (Bookbinders) Ltd, King's Lynn, Norfolk

This book is sold subject to the condition that it shall not, by way of trade or otherwise, be lent, re-sold, hired out, or otherwise circulated without the publisher's prior consent in any form of binding or cover other than that in which it is published and without a similar condition including this condition being imposed on the subsequent purchaser.

ISBN-13   978-0-9551370-0-6   ISBN-10   0-9551370-0-4

Creative Writing: the Matrix
Exercises & Ideas for Creative Writing Teachers

Contents
88 Exercises, 7 Writer's Toolkits, 21 Mini-Lectures

Introduction iv
Guide to using this book v
Cheat's Index and About Using Extracts vi

Section 1. NURTURE: A Safe Place in Which to Grow
    I   Mapping the Course 3
    II   Forming and Supporting the Group 6

Section 2. STIMULUS: Sparking the Writer
    I   Essentials 19
    II   25 Further Sparking Exercises 29
    III   Pairing Devices & Exercises 40
    IV   End-of-Course Fun and Games 43

Section 3. CRAFT: Producing the Work
    I   Story 49
    II   Character 53
    III   Point of View 57
    IV   Dialogue 60
    V   Scene and Plot 64
    VI   Storytelling Devices 77
    VII Deeper into Character 81
    VIII Richer Writing 83
    IX   Dip into Poetry 91
    X   Fixing a Story 94

Section 4. PROCESS: Living the Writing Life
    I   Teaching Writing/Growing People 99
    II   Into the Writing World 116

Section 5. RUNNING THE COURSE: Enriching Elements
    I   Workshopping 125
    II   Using a Class Text 129
    III   Managing Discussions 130
    IV   Sensitive Flowers & Other Pitfalls 132
    V   Feedback, Tutorials & Assignments (or Not) 133

Sources 137

MATRIX, according to the Concise Oxford Dictionary, means 'womb; place in which thing is developed.' Which feels to me exactly what a creative writing class is – a place to develop.

To tutors reading this book: I've written Creative Writing: the Matrix for you with the assumption that you are a writer. Maybe you are published, even much published, maybe still working toward that glorified state. Some of my writerly explanations may seem simplistic – sorry about that, but it's because I've learned students need these basics. Some, on the other hand, may seem scanty – because I assume that you know what I mean and you'll use your knowledge, experience and creativity to fill in the gaps. Ditto teaching: if you're an old hand, you'll gut this book for what you need – we're always looking for new material, aren't we! I have started, however, with the notion that you are new to the role of creative writing tutor – welcome to the front of the classroom.

To writers reading this book: Aha, a how-to addict! You'll be looking, as always, for insights and methods to help you write. A lot of the exercises here are adapted for teaching from books aimed at writers, so you may be able to interpret them backwards for work on your own – or use the source list to buy the originals. However, most exercises need leadership, many only succeed as staged or surprise writing, quite a few need pairs or groupwork, many need preparation – now you see what your tutor does for you! If you're in a writers' circle, members in turn can take on the ringmaster role to run exercises. I wish you good writing.

About Susan Lee Kerr

After a BA degree with a major in English Literature in the United States I won a Mademoiselle Magazine Guest Editorship which lead to my first job, as a copywriter at Condé Nast Publishing. In London in the 80s I became a freelance feature writer for women's magazines, then wrote two self-help books published by Hodder & Stoughton, began teaching adult creative writing and embarked on writing poetry and fiction, a journey that continues. For ten years I was a board member and then chair of Women Writers Network in London; I was Course Team Leader for Journalism, Media & Creative Writing at Richmond Adult Community College and still teach, having accumulated some 29,000 student hours of teaching.

Why this book? Writing has been my life, and I love helping people to find their own voices. I've taught all the exercises and mini-lectures, discovered and used all the ideas in this book. They're tried, tested, tweaked and true, and it seems the next right thing is to share my experience with others.

A guide to using Creative Writing: The Matrix Exercises & Ideas for Creative Writing Teachers

This book is arranged in five sections which are not necessarily to be read in order, and certainly not to be used in consecutive order when teaching a creative writing course for adults. Sections 1 and 5, *Nurture* and *Running the Course,* include suggestions on overall planning and organising, along with some exercises, ideas and mini-lectures. Sections 2, 3, 4 *Stimulus, Craft* and *Process* feature loads of exercises and mini-lectures.

The craft focus is prose fiction and narrative, applicable to short story, possibly novel, possibly memoir. Poetry, drama, screenplays, journalism get no attention, or else just passing mentions – they deserve their own books. However, *Process, Stimulus* and the organising sections contain much that applies to all forms of creative writing.

I am indebted to the authors of the how-to books from which I have adapted exercises and mini-lectures; I credit them by mention on the page, and list details in *Sources,* and urge readers to seek the originals. I credit, too, creative writing tutors of courses I've attended.

Italics throughout the book indicate instructions for you (tutor) to give to students; obviously not meant as a verbatim script, this lets me shortcut explanations.

Arial generally means that I suggest you write the key points on the board and/or make the information into a handout or tasksheet to go with the lesson.

For ease of using the book as a reference I've numbered the exercises, mini-lectures and writer's toolkits – but this in no way indicates order for use in the class. Skip around, pick and choose; call on your own creativity for class planning.

Cheat's Index

Because exercises and mini-lectures are numbered and subsections are listed on contents page, a complete index seems unnecessary. However, a few scattered general categories which you may want to find quickly include...

Exercise methods (types of):
    bubbling 19-24, listing 24-26, postcards & pictures 35-37,
    staged 38, pairing/matching 40-42, small group 57, 69

One-day classes 3, 10, 11, 40, 135

Negativity 19, 29, 34, 39, 105-108, 111, 132-3

No preparation 13, 30, 39-40, 51,132

Poetry 24, 37, 38, 47, 91-94

Questionnaires 8-10, 136

Tutor tips 24, 53, 69, 121, 132

Section	Exercises	Mini Lectures	Writer's Toolkits	See Pages
1. Nurture	1 – 4	1		3 –16
2. Stimulus	5 – 45	2	1 – 2	19 – 44
3. Craft	46 – 84	3 – 12		47 – 95
4. Process	85 – 88	13 – 20	1 – 7	99 –122
5. Running the Course		21		125–136

About using extracts in teaching

'Some actions which would be infringements of copyright in other circumstances are legal when taken for educational purposes – but the limits are rigid,' warns the Handbook of Copyright in British Publishing Practice. If in doubt, consult this book via The Society of Authors or similar establishment. Also, most educational institutions hold an agreement with the Copyright Licensing Agency (CLA); check the guidelines displayed by copying machines. In general, according to both of the above, if you are working at a recognised educational establishment you may reproduce or adapt and copy without permission so long as you do it only for instruction. This may include up to one complete chapter from a book, one article from a magazine, a short story or poem (not more than 10 pages) from an anthology or 5% of the publication, if greater than these. The CLA licence does not cover newspapers.

Section 1

NURTURE: A safe place in which to grow

I. Mapping the Course

II. Forming and Supporting the Group

Section 1

NURTURE: A Safe Place in Which to Grow

I. MAPPING THE COURSE

When you sit down to prepare a course, 12 weeks, 30 weeks, 6 weeks or even one day feels a daunting acreage to fill. You may want to theme each session or you may want to just coast but in my experience teaching is easier and students are happier when there's structure to each class, and to the course as a whole. You don't have to set it in stone or even type and hand it out, but do sketch out a plan for yourself, and even if only verbal, give the class a notion of direction – it gives energy to the course.

This *Nurture* section provides a course planning and pacing overview, and then suggests specifics for the first class of a course. *Stimulus, Craft* and *Process* sections follow with heaps of material to piece together to suit your own style and class needs. Then ***Running the Course*** gives further elements for teaching creative writing, including workshopping, discussions, text analysis and assignments.

Planning a one day course. This book is written for courses lasting weeks or months, but you may find yourself doing one-day or weekend courses. You might focus on the elements of story writing using stimulus exercises, or you could plan a close-up day on just one craft aspect, like character or dialogue. Good pacing is vital; see suggestions for single sessions below.

Planning a long course. For a beginners' general creative writing course you'll work through a range of disciplines – short story, poetry, radio and/or stage play, lifewriting, perhaps articles or children's stories. My main focus in this book is the intermediate or advanced prose course covering the narrative skills in Section 3, *Craft.* Whatever the content, break the stretch of weeks into mini-series (say dialogue or character) dotted with one-offs (see *Stimulus*). Language-enriching wordplay (in *Craft)* linked to nothing at all is a good livener any time; sprinkle in some *Process* here and there. Schedule discussion and lecture sessions sparingly. And do try in every single meeting to get students' pen to paper – it's a writing class! (And a few students may never write anywhere but in the classroom, alas.)

Over the length of a course, ring the changes among the **individual writing exercises** you choose (all of these are described in this book): stimulus from picture, word, object, situation, character... from a **variety of instructions:** taskslip, worksheet or peer imperative, multi-staged, transcribing, listing, bubbling...

Remember to vary methods of **class participation** detailed along with specific activities in this book: pairing devices (see end of *Stimulus* section), groupwork (see **Agony Letter** and **Groupwork Scene Writing** in *Craft),* paired discussion (see *Running the Course).*

Plan each session. A successful class comes from a variety of activities of differing paces, in chunks of 10, 15 or 20 minutes each. You need to balance quiet 'down' activities (individual writing exercises, reading out or workshopping, occasional mini-lectures) with lively 'up' work (pairs or groups, whole-group report-backs, pooled discussion). A whole two hours, or a whole day, in just one of these modes leaves everyone dissatisfied. So plan your session, and be the time keeper, wrapping up and moving on to the next activity, keeping energy levels strong.

A secret of good teaching is... not teaching. Don't TELL students, LET them learn, especially by leading them to participate (writing, talking, reading out). Some telling is inevitable, but try always to have an active writing stimulus to kick off a lecturey topic, eg dialogue.

Don't cling to the front of the classroom. In pair or group activities stroll about listening in, lightly supervising to keep students to the task, answering questions, picking up points to make to the whole class when you regroup.

Another not-teaching essential: coffee break. Education studies have shown that peak attention lasts for 20 minutes, then begins to fade (hence the need for changes of pace, above). So good teaching practice REQUIRES a break at around one hour (or 90 minutes for a 3 hour session). The studies show that on return to the classroom attention is high again. There's more to this than refreshment, too. If you have been

CREATIVE WRITING CLASS PLAN

Session 1 **Term** 1 **Date** 15/9/2010 **Tutor:** *Susan Kerr*

Contents/Topic: *Overview, Introductions & Warming Up to Writing*

Learning Outcome/Objective:
- *To map the course and own goals*
- *To strengthen writing confidence*

Time/Duration		Tutor/Student Activities	Resources
7:00	15	Arrival activities	Starting Points Questionnaire
			Index cards; place-name cards
			Browsing Materials
			Whiteboard
7:15	10	Welcome; announcements	
		Overview of today's session	
7:25	15	Introduction briefing	Pair cards (words)
		Mini-interviews (pairs)	Task on whiteboard
	15	Introduce partners to group	
7:55	10	BREAK	

(really it will be 15 minutes minimum before all are back and settled, but try for ten)

8:10	10	Introduce myself	
		Map of the course	Handout
8:20	5	Group Bubble Demo	Whiteboard
	5 + 10	Rock, Scissors, Paper	
		– individuals Bubble & Write	
	15	Volunteers read out	
8:55	5	Any questions; reminders and advice.	

an adult student, you'll know the break reinforces the teaching. Students continue to talk about what they've just been doing in class; even in social chat they continue the bonding and support fellow-writers need. Try to keep break to 10 minutes… but it always takes longer. A further tip: after break is a good time for 'class business' announcements or perhaps a mini-lecture. Start of class is NOT good for this, due to late-arrivers, but at the midway restart everybody's present and fully alert.

II. FORMING AND SUPPORTING THE GROUP

It is the first session. No matter how advanced the writer – or how new to writing – everyone likes to feel good about being creative. And no one likes feeling anxious or criticized. As tutor, your initial job is to create a friendly, supportive and competent atmosphere. Confidence is the key to successful growth in creative writing, and you build it right from the start. Here's my established plan for a first class.

Preparation: class plan. Create a plan format on your pc, print out a blank and complete by hand – you can type if you like, but I prefer the organic feel. I find no two sessions are ever identical, especially as the course goes on, so there's little use in keeping typed plans in my doc files. Sitting down with the blank form helps focus my energies on the particular class, and reminds me what materials to bring.

I put the plan in a clear plastic looseleaf page with my class notes and materials and take it out of the binder for class so I can glance and prompt myself as to what's supposed to happen next. It's amazing how your wits can fly out the window once you're talking and interacting with students. Of course the times are notional; be ever ready to adapt to circumstances – fewer or too many students, queries, room changes, admin tangles, any of these can throw your timing. Keep calm and soldier on cheerfully – you and your writers are here to enjoy writing.

Preparation: browsing materials. People will arrive early, late and in between for the first class, so you can't start on the dot. But the silence as they gather is awkward, so prepare a selection of eye-openers and support from the writing world:

- writing magazines (back-dated is fine)
- writing 'bibles' (Writer's Handbook, Writers' & Artists' Yearbook)
- competition fliers
- fliers for author readings, writing events, residential courses
- if available, a binder containing previous students' published work
- possibly samples of your own published work

Preparation: whiteboard & tutor kit. Write <u>Welcome</u> and the name of the class on the board to focus students and let them know they're in the right place. Therefore – your tutor kit: a pencil case or pouch containing dry-wipe board marker, paper towelling cloth (because there is never a board eraser when you need one), gummy picture-tack and sticky-tape (to put up signs when your classroom is suddenly moved). Also handy: some spare pens (yes, students sometimes come to a writing class without writing materials), a small pair of scissors, some paper clips.

Preparation: other materials. I assume you know the following, but just to be sure…

- handout – a sheet of information tutor prepares in advance and photocopies to give to all students; it's good to use coloured paper for essentials you want them to keep throughout a course. Or just to liven things up!

- worksheet and questionnaire – a full page photocopied handout that the student writes on in class

- tasksheet or taskslip – a half sheet or strip of paper tutor has prepared in advance and cut up for distribution as part of an exercise.

Preparation: room arrangement has a huge impact. Feng shui or whatever, it affects the way the tutor leads and students bond, vital for forming the group into a nurturing environment. Get to the room 10 – 15 minutes before class starts, especially for the first session, to move furniture if necessary.

A hollow square is probably the most satisfying arrangement: students on three sides of a square or rectangle, tutor's desk at the centre of the fourth side. This way everyone has good sightlines and hearing access, and you can make eye contact with each student.

Boardroom-style around a rectangular table can work, a big round table even better, for a group of up to twelve. Worst scenario is row-on-row so that people are looking at the back of people's heads – this gives a feeling of loneliness, competition and teacher-knows-best. You want to create a group of co-crafters, a writers' circle with writing table space.

START OF COURSE ACTIVITY

In the ten minutes you allow for people to straggle in, provide useful activity. The **browsing materials,** as above, and:

Small index cards – ask for name, address, telephone, email (write these instructions on board). This is your tutor file, in case you need to contact students (to see why they are not attending perhaps, or if you have to cancel a class). For a 1-day class, you might just ask for name, and an indication of a writing interest or worry.

Large index cards – as students return the small cards to you, fold a 5" x 8" index card lengthwise, and print their preferred first name on it in large letters. Quiet banter as you do this helps you get to know each student by name. Students put their cards at their places for the benefit of all. Use these for the first couple of weeks of class so people get to know each other.

1 EXERCISE: Start of course questionnaire

Now this may sound school-like, but a start-of-course form is extremely useful to the tutor AND it gives students an engaging activity to help them settle in. Suggested questions:

STARTING POINTS

1. In order of priority, list the kinds of writing you prefer to do, and would like to work on this year (for example, short story, novel, memoir, feature articles...). If you have equal priorities, or more priorities, adjust the list.

    1. _____

    2. _____

    3. _____

2. If you have a keen specialty or genre writing preference (thriller, romance, historical, children's etc), please specify.

3. How long have you been writing, what creative writing classes have you taken (or other participation, such as writers' groups)?

4. Describe your writing progress and how you feel about it.

5. Describe some of your writing needs and goals. How do you hope this course can help you?

6. Do you want to submit work for publication? Do you know where to submit? Or are you already submitting (if so, where, what results)?

7. List 2 books (and their authors) you have read and enjoyed recently.

Feel free to continue answers or make further comments/requests over page.

Tutor, make this a full page, with space for student name at top, and room after each question so students can answer in short jottings on the sheet.

Questionnaire feedback. You can see that you'll learn a lot about the writing level of the students, their interests and needs, which will help you pitch the tone, level and contents of your course. After you've analysed the questionnaires at home, summarise and feed back to the class in the next session. This lets them know they've been heard; besides, they're curious and it's an aid to the bonding of the group. For a one day class, interests and needs written on the small index card serves the same purpose. You can also short-cut to a simple show of hands.

INTRODUCTION EXERCISES

Now that all are gathered, give the briefest of welcomes, identifying yourself, the course and the session's plan and vital announcements (when is the coffee break, where are the toilets and emergency exit), but don't launch into lecture mode. Instead, begin the warming and bonding process immediately with creative introductions. Here are several tried and true possibilities. Take notes yourself during each introduction and keep this list, to aid your memorisation of names, facts, faces of your students.

2 EXERCISE: Mini interviews in pairs

Lively and creative ways to pair people suggested later in **Pairing Devices**; here's the task, which is structured and writing-related. Italics throughout this book indicate instructions you (tutor) give to students, so italicised *you* means students. *The writing rationale here is practice at interview technique and sharpening curiosity – good tools for all writers. Interview each other on the points below, with a view to introducing your partner to the class, so you must take notes. Five minutes each to ask each other's*

- *Name*
- *Occupation (past or present) or, if preferred, a passion, hobby or interest*
- *Stage of writing, or why taking the class*

As they talk, write reminders of the task on the board. Keep an eye on the time; give a one-minute warning before they have to switch roles, so they're sure to cover the points; then time the next five minutes in the same way.

Interview time's up, back to a big group, and now go round the room as each person introduces his or her partner and a few of the facts gained. This method makes everyone a star for a few moments and gives everyone at least one friend in the class.

3 EXERCISE: Self-introductions

Though inclined to make people feel self-conscious, individual self-introductions are simple and straightforward, and the most efficient method for a one day course. To set a model of brevity, you might want to introduce yourself first (see below on tutor introduction). Or just tell them to keep it brief, and perhaps put task prompts on the board.

4 EXERCISE: Name game

A mode of individual self-introduction, but more creative: *Print your first name in large letters down centre of a page, then use the letters as a sort of acrostic, making words that describe yourself... or your writing. For example, Concise-Lazy-Artistic-Rhythm-English.*

Then go round the room using these as introductions. **Variation:** ... how you <u>wish</u> you or your writing would be described. This fantasy version is more entertaining and warming as individuals introduce themselves.

1 MINI-LECTURE: Course Overview

After the round of introductions and coffee break, you're well into the always rather shaggy first session of a course. The key point is that the students are warmed to each other and have begun to feel comfortable as a group. This is the time to talk AT them. Tell them about yourself (more on this below), assure them that we'll be doing some writing today shortly, but first, an overview of the course. Make clear that the plan is flexible, will adapt to their needs, and – because we are creatives here – it may change, but overall, here's the map. You might say something like:

We'll look at character first, because all story comes from character. We'll cover scene and structure, and dialogue, of course. In term 2 (or 'later in the course') I'll cover how to present and submit your work, we'll spend some time on the processes of the writing life... and so on.

Vague? Yes, but you are suggesting a pathway, yet remaining open to adjustments (especially as you look over those start-of-course questionnaires, and take a similar survey mid-way through a long course). Ask if there are any burning needs, any questions at this stage; if any require long-winded answers try to reassure students that these will be covered – but now we have to get writing.

WRITING AND READING OUT

Writing kick-off. Finally, the point of it all: get the class down to pen-on-paper. Some may be timid, but, really, everyone wants to write, and wants to be made to write. A demonstration of **Bubbling** and then **Choose One** are my favourite starters, because they ease people into in-class writing. See the next section, *Stimulus,* for these exercises (because they can be used many times, with variations, during a course). Emphasise that these are just for fun, to limber up creatively, nobody need worry.

To read out or not to read out? For the first session you may want to assure a very new-to-writing group that they won't have to read out today. Conversely, you may find that newcomers or more experienced writers are desperately keen to read out. (See **On Reading Out,** below.) However many readers you have, this first class is NOT the time to invite critique from others, nor for you to criticise. At the start, students look to tutor-as-god, so speak only praise for now and, like Bambi's Thumper, 'if you don't have nuthin' nice to say, then don't say it at all.' Do praise anything that is particularly strong and good, opening out to useful generalisations, about using the senses, for instance, or attention to concrete detail, or good characterisation.

Wrap-up. Invite students to take this little piece home to polish and type to give you next week, if they would like individual feedback. By now class time is probably up... if there's 5 - 10 minutes to spare you can encourage questions at large... or suggest individuals come forward to speak to you at your desk... or tell students to write for 5 minutes on their response to today's class. This kind of reflective writing for student's private self is always a good fallback if you are stuck with extra time in any class – and it is NOT wasted; we all could do with more pauses in which to record and integrate our experiences, especially when learning.

ON READING OUT

The description above is for the first session, but ever afterwards your students will be reading out for critical feedback from tutor and peers. The tone and attitude of criticism in your class is crucial to your course's success. Right from the start make clear that comments should be constructive, not destructive, that we are here to support each other as writers. Students also need guidance on how to read out and how to accept criticism. In the very first session I convey this by brief mention and general attitude; I think the second session is better for getting to the nitty-gritty of critique. In Section 5, *Running the Course,* I describe formal workshopping, suitable for intermediate and advanced writers who bring in completed drafts. Over the page are guidelines for quickie readings after exercises, given as a handout. You may prefer to deliver these simply as an informal mini-lecture if the handout feels too rule-bound.

Reading out, the tutor as ringmaster. Try not to be the first to critique every time – students expect you to be the voice of wisdom, but they must learn that their responses can be equally valid. If one critique goes on too long, ask another student for an opinion, or bring up another point of consideration. Encourage many, watching to see who almost speaks, but is crossed over by another – come back to call on the almost-speaker. It is good too for the tutor to disagree with some comments, good to leave points open-ended. Refer back to the author – 'Well, Sally will have to make up her mind about that.'

Suggestions on Reading Out, Commenting and Receiving Criticism

You as the Reader

1. Read loud and proud – sit up straight, project voice outward.

2. Let your piece stand with the briefest of preambles, or none at all. Don't apologise, and never say it's probably just rubbish. Class exercises are not meant to be perfect.

You as a Critiquer

1. Always open with a positive comment – 'I liked the detail about the meal.' 'The little boy is totally convincing.'... Come back to positives now and then: what works well?

2. Don't be bland and nice. When you don't like something, don't hold back, but don't use generalities ('It just doesn't work'). Try, 'I got confused where...' "I needed to know more about....'

3. Be specific in your comments (opening, motivation, action etc), but include general issues like pace, shape, tone.

4. Comment on actions and thoughts of 'the narrator', 'the speaker' or 'the character', not the writer. Do NOT assume that because the author writes so vividly about drink, drugs or divorce that it is his/her own experience. Try to keep a distance, so that we are free to write without personal exposure.

5. Keep to the work at hand. Interesting as it may be, don't relate your own similar experiences. And don't take over the work and say how to rewrite it your way. Be open to types of writing that may not be your personal cup of tea.

6. Don't harp on one particular point. If your criticism has been covered, just say you agree and pass on to something else.

You, Receiving Criticism

1. Just listen and absorb, not rising to each point or question. Remember that this is only a quick, rough exercise, that nothing is perfect at first go, that writing is re-writing.

2. Explain or clarify, but try not to get defensive. Always bear in mind that the criticism is of the work on the page, not of you personally.

3. Don't do anything about the criticism immediately. Let it sink in, mull it over. Let yourself recover perspective. After a few days you'll know better which comments to heed, which to dismiss – this is YOUR work. It may help to write a defense or response if something really rankles – this is to keep to yourself, and look at a few weeks later. As you get to know a group, you'll learn particular preferences of some individuals which may help you weigh their criticism more readily.

Occasionally, vary the methods of reading out after exercises. Going round the room one-by-one can get tedious and take too long. Sometimes just ask for, say, four volunteer readers-out, then move on to your next activity. Or let everyone have an airing by sharing with a neighbour or small group – this is especially useful if you have a large class.

TUTOR GROUND RULES & SUPPORT

Plenty of nurture for students in this chapter – now what about you? Here are some general tips and ground rules – others supplied with exercises as we go along, and see Section 5, *Running the Course* as well.

- You are in the business of building confidence. As detailed above, praise first, criticise after, identifying specifics. Then try to sum up with praise.

- Respect the writing silence. Do not rustle about with the register or busywork as students write an exercise. You communicate amazing strength and belief in them when you simply sit and be still as they write. Only exception – if you write the exercise along with them.

- Avoid tutor-as-god fallacy. Students hope you have all the answers and some magic as well. This inevitability (especially with beginners) must be gradually converted to tutor-as-peer. Sure, you're ahead in the game, but your task is to grow the students into a peer group who trust each others' judgement.

- Guard yourself. Students will be delighted to eat up all your attention. Do not give out your home telephone or address, do not invite students to your house, do not take home bumper quantities of student writing, do not make special appointments out of class. You teach in your teaching time, you give feedback on writing at regular intervals, but you must not let yourself be put in the position of writing expert who will care for a student every step of the way. Make this clear, or your own writing time and personal life risks invasion. Do tell students how they can get a message to you; email is brilliant, of course, because you can answer it when you choose. I keep a separate email address for student contact. Keep up your barriers, avoid the temptation to slip into e-dialogues – you aren't paid for out-of-hours work; you need your time and energies for yourself. Also see **Sensitive Flowers** in *Running the Course* section.

- Limit tutor's star turn. Of course the students long to know what and how you write – but don't let your ego take over. In the introductions, sketch in your writing path and current activities briefly; they have a right to know. If you participate in an exercise you may choose to read out – only IF there's time, IF all have read before you. At some point they may ask you to read something of your own work – once a year is plenty – this is their course. Invite their critiques of your work.

- I've found that teaching creative writing is one third knowledge, one third nurture and one third entertainment – keep on surprising students and they'll keep on being stimulated, keep on writing.

On with the course! Now that you have structure and pacing in mind, writing exercises, the fuel of your teaching, follow in the *Stimulus, Craft* and *Process* sections. *Running the Course* provides a guide to other components of the creative writing class.

Section 2

STIMULUS: Sparking the writer

I. Essentials

II. 25 Further Sparking Exercises

III. Pairing Devices & Exercises

IV. End-of-Course Fun and Games

Section 2

STIMULUS: Sparking the Writer

Like the young Colette, I need a Willy... he locked her in a room and wouldn't let her out until she had produced some writing. Would that I had such a task master, just as your students want YOU to make THEM write. But bullying won't work. Instead you need to light the spark, indeed sometimes to coax it.

At early stages, despite signing up for class, many students are frozen in fear, inhibited, stuck in formalities, even generally resistant or cynically negative. So you need to ease them into their creativity. See *Nurture* and *Process* for more about this.

Beginners aren't the only students who need stimulus. At any time throughout a course, at any level, students want sparking to seed a new project, to enrich their word-power or simply to write for fun.

I. Essentials

Three early stimulus musts are **Writer's Toolkits 1 and 2,** and the mini-lecture **Writing with the 8 Senses** with its writing follow-ups. There are some 45 other exercises in this section to use throughout your course. However, an excess of stimulus writing can result in lots of promising work done in class... but no follow-up. I don't think it is creatively healthy for students to get hooked on writing-as-parlour-games; they've got to learn to expand, complete, polish, finish. So use these (usually quick, 15-20 minutes) exercises judiciously.

What to do with the results in class? Normally, read out and share the creativity (see **Writing and Reading Out**, in *Nurture* section), so I have not described that stage in all the exercises below.

WRITER'S TOOLKIT 1: Bubble Chart

First in a series of seven essential writing process tools to introduce to all writers.

This is ideal as the very first writing exercise. There are variations: school kids are taught to spider chart, brain specialist Tony Buzan invented the term mindmapping, Gabriel Luser Rico calls it clustering, Henriette Anne Klauser says branching, business people might say brainstorming on paper – I dub it bubbling, and avoid formal rules. Bubbling is a fail-safe way to tackle any project or problem at any stage. Stuck with a small idea? This expands, fans the spark. Overwhelmed by too many possibilities? This tames, works towards an order. Do it for yourself at home to see how it operates if you don't already know.

Demonstrating to the class is stronger than just telling, so put a concrete word in the centre of the white board. Ask the class to call out any thing they associate with the word and write around the circled central word. Draw lines out, sprawl, and only worry about grouping concepts if the association is instant. Example:

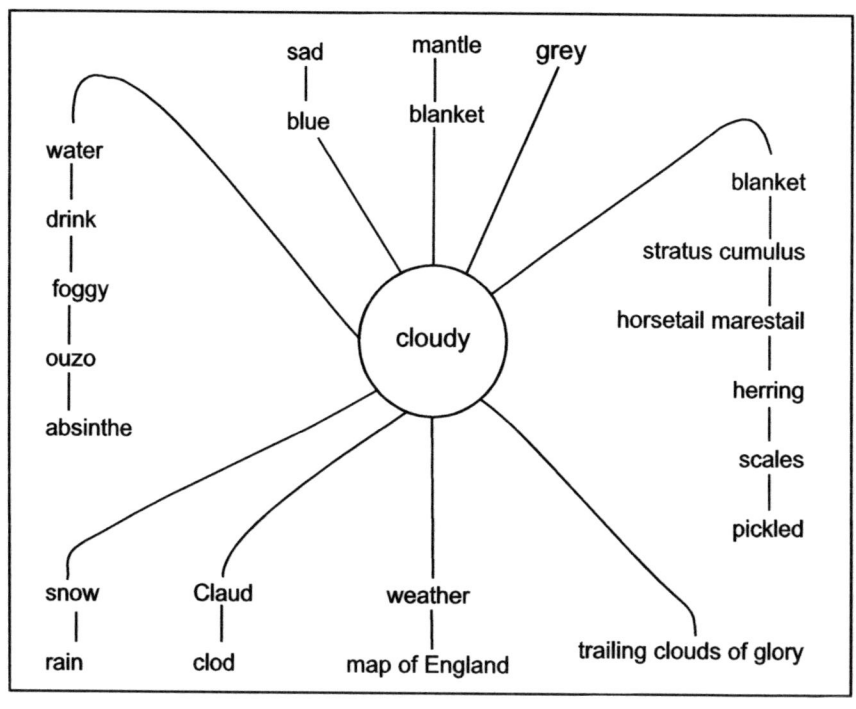

```
                    sad      mantle     grey
                     |         |         /
                    blue     blanket
        water                                    blanket
         |                                         |
        drink                                  stratus cumulus
         |                                         |
        foggy                                  horsetail marestail
         |         ( cloudy )                     |
        ouzo                                    herring
         |                                         |
        absinthe                                 scales
                                                   |
                                                 pickled
        snow      Claud      weather
         |         |           |
        rain      clod     map of England    trailing clouds of glory
```

Once the students have shared this as a whole group they do it individually. Make them position their paper horizontally, the better to think laterally. I sometimes give out unlined sheets of paper to encourage non-logic. (See *Process* section, **Right Brain/Left Brain** for how and why bubbling works.)

Proffer round your **Word Box** (see further on in *Stimulus*). They choose a word at random... and bubble for 5 minutes or so. Urge them not to worry, just jot anywhere on page as the ideas come, write big or little, use branching lines, circles or just words, even draw little pictures, maybe connect with lines or arrows.

What's the point? Someone always asks. To get free, to expand, to explore, to get away from confined, frozen thinking. Most students are startled and amazed by the joy of freedom in this exercise.

Next, for start-of-course, go into the exercise **Choose One, Bubble & Riff** ahead. But you can also bubble with **Word Box,** an exercise a bit further on, and see *Craft* section for applications to prose and poetry. In fact, once you've introduced this basic tool, you'll use it often. Remind students to bubble as they start almost any exercise. Tell them: *bubbling is a method, a strategy to use any time.* At home they can bubble-chart away from the desk: sit on floor, sprawl on bed, take over dining table – free that creativity!

WRITER'S TOOLKIT 2: Chaos Writing
An essential writing process tool to introduce to all writers.

This is an extraordinary method for getting into writing which I first encountered in Henriette Anne Klauser's book Writing on Both Sides of the Brain. It works on any project, at any stage of the writing life. Called freewriting, rapidwriting, hot penning, chaos writing, nonstop, nonlinear, junque, garbage (pronounced garbahjjjj)... it is described and recommended in many how-to-write books.

If you teach only bubbling **(Writer's Toolkit 1)** and chaos writing in a one-day class you'll have given students the access to their creativity. You must, of course, try it for yourself at home if it is entirely new to you. In a longer course with all the getting-to-know-you essentials you'll have to leave chaos writing to the second or third session, because it takes about 30 minutes altogether. Explain chaos writing very briefly as above and tell students, *You are now about to do it here – these are the rules...*

WRITER'S TOOLKIT: CHAOS WRITING

- *You will write for 10 minutes without stopping NO ONE WILL READ THIS OR SEE IT BUT YOU. I'll give you a starting phrase, I will watch the clock; you just start writing whatever comes into your head, or out of your hand.*
- *You can –*
    stray from the subject and come back to it
    write about how you are feeling – anxious, angry, bored, exhilarated
    be ungrammatical, leave out commas, spell things wrong, think of the exact word later, or write all the near approximates, ignore logical meaning, make giant leaps of thought – just keep on
    be silly or stupid or playful or exaggerated – keep writing fast: flow
- *if you feel embarrassed or silly, write about it;*
- *if you feel some tension in your body write that – tight lips or throat, cramp*
- *if you want to stop, write that in too, but keep on writing and go on maybe to say how much you want to stop*
- *try not to think, let your hand do it; a semitrance*
- *if you sense a break in the unthinking flow write yourself through it or try repeating the last spontaneous word until the nonlogical surge starts up again*
- *no lists or logical thoughts allowed, but if you suddenly remember you have to get the dry cleaning write it in and keep going*
- *if something happens in the room or out the window or in the hall, and it distracts you, write about that. JUST DON'T STOP.*
- *At some point, perhaps not now but when you do a 20 minute chaos writing session on your own, you will encounter THE BLOCK. You dry up, have absolutely nothing more to say. Mark this spot, or write about it, but tell yourself you will go on – just 5 minutes more, or to the bottom of the page, or till tutor says stop. If nothing else, try writing the last spontaneous word over and over. This applies not only to chaos writing, but all kinds of writing. Usually a nugget of gold, or a whole vein, lies beyond.*

Now give the starting phrase, and as tutor, just listen, watch and feel the whoosh of their release. **Starting phrase:** *When I try to write I feel...*
   Tutor's role is to clockwatch and announce when the 10 minutes is up. Allow another minute for people to finish a thought or jot next thoughts. When time's up and students return to this world shaking out cramped hands and expressing surprise at the journey they've travelled, explain some of the uses of chaos writing – but not beforehand. Students must experience it first, without a 'purpose' to freeze their writing.

What's the point? Tell students they are not to read this for a few days or even longer – or they needn't read it at all. Chaos writing is a wonderful tool for exploring a problem, in this instance feelings about writing. It also works for letting off steam about a specific writing problem or a difficult work or life situation. There are a few practical uses for chaos writing – given later in *Stimulus* and *Process* – but the main point is to experience writing with critical faculties turned off.

5 EXERCISE: Choose One, Bubble & Riff

This is my favourite for launching writers, even experienced ones. First you must demonstrate **Toolkit 1: Bubble Chart,** with the group as a whole. Then write a list on the board, and tell students to choose one word from the list and bubble it. Three different list suggestions:

- Rock, Scissors, Paper
- Earth, Air, Fire, Water
- Red, Blue, Yellow

After five minutes tell students to stop, to look over their now busy sheet of paper, and to choose one word, phrase or area that appeals most... and now write on further: a paragraph or a half-page or so... whatever they feel like writing. Explore wherever it takes them, this time in sentences, not just single words. Allow 5 - 10 minutes for this.

What's the point? These little pieces, called vignettes by Gabriele Lusser Rico in Writing the Natural Way, can simply be left as that – little prose riffs, pieces good for the pleasure of doing more than for any further purpose. For class, this is enough. For tutors or students who demand more, some variations on uses of riffs:

- if done as a series on a theme, they could be polished and patterned together, say like Michèle Roberts Une Glossaire in *During Mother's Absence*
- instead of prose, the riff stage can be done as poetry
- riffs can springboard into a story, memoir piece or feature
- if students want feedback, they can hand in the riff-piece to you, or they can take it home to type, polish and hand in at next class

TIP: List, Bubble & Riff Forever. I use variations on this exercise throughout the course. You can drop it in any time you need a quick stimulus or filler for a sudden blank in your class plan. Or focus it to suit a theme, or as an adjunct to a craft series.

6 EXERCISE: More Bubble & Riff Stimuli

Instead of a word, try some of these starters suggested by Rico...

- Sounds: Sh, Fl, Th, M etc
- Letters: any letter of the alphabet, perhaps alphabetically around the room
- Emotions: afraid... angry... joy...
- Objects: see **Serendipity Bag**

7 EXERCISE: Life-Listing

This is a particularly good way to get students into their own private store of writing sparks. In two stages, the process stirs, then stirs again, allowing the writer to discover more to say than he or she thought possible.

Stage 1. *List six objects you remember from childhood.* (Someone will ask, I usually say under the age of ten). Give 5 minutes for this; if some get only to three or four that's fine.

Stage 2. *Sit back, study the list. Choose one to write on, the one that speaks to you most at this moment. Another time it might be another one, but right now, choose one and start writing. You might want to bubble first, or maybe it's ready to come flowing out, just write. A paragraph is fine, more if you want to.* Allow 10, 15 or even 20 minutes for this.

What's the point? These can be left as riffs only, or they can be a springboard to evocative short stories, poems or plays. Students are often amazed at the excellence of their own and their classmates' pieces.

8 EXERCISE: More Listing-and-Riffs Stimuli

You can use this powerful exercise many times over, in many ways. It can lead to deep, true and sometimes funny personal 'epiphanies', into life-writing (memoir, personal feature articles) or into fiction. Some ways in: *List six*

- Childhood favourite articles of clothing (or unfavourite)
- Childhood foods (or food from any stage of life)
- People from childhood
- Places from childhood (geographical places, or rooms)
- Things you would save from a fire in your home
- Favourite films (or books)

9 EXERCISE: Life-Listing in Depth variation

Childhood pulls out strong material, but surprisingly rich stuff comes of other periods, too. This is a multi-staged exercise in which you dictate categories and age-range. You can work through it over a one year course, as small stimuli, or use it intensively in 6-week, one-day or weekend courses focussing on life-writing.

Stage 1. **Tutor, start by dictating ONE category to the students:**
- Objects or items OR places OR people
- **Then dictate ONE age-range:**
- Under age 10
- Age 10 or 12 to 16 or 18 (adolescence, teen years)
- Age 18 – early, mid 20s (first setting out, setting up)

Stage 2. **Give students 5 minutes to list at one category and age-range,** for instance, *List 5-10 people you remember from age 12-17, your adolescent years.*

Stage 3. **Then stop the listing, and announce** another age-range, say, *People remembered from under age 10.*

Stage 4. **After 5 minutes of listing,** move students on. *List people from your early 20s.*

Stage 5. **Now students look over their lists.** *Choose one person to describe and expand on, bubble and write a paragraph or page.*

The results, if developed into longer work, might be by theme – people or a person vividly recalled over all those growing up years, or the importance of place to the writer. If you work through the entire exercise students might develop a long piece about the objects, people and places in one time-period.

MINI-LECTURE 2: Writing with the 8 Senses

This absolutely essential element of creative writing works with almost any writing stimulus. Use it early on to get people writing vividly.

Ask students to call out the senses; write them on the whiteboard as they do so. The obvious will come first, and then I point out three others I've identified. Then delve deeper into each via lecture, at first.

As a demonstration, I like to halt everything for a whole long minute so we all listen: the hum of a computer, talk in the corridor, drone of a plane, rev of an engine, one's own breathing... Invite your students to stretch their senses, augmenting the list on the board:

Sound – *peel off layers of sound*

Taste – *temperature and feel of food in the mouth, nuances, memories (and as smell)*

Smell – *familiar, unknown, indescribable (new combinations of familiar)*

Sight – *panorama, close-up, middle distance; above, below; colour, texture, shape, pattern; straight, curved, angular; banish the word beautiful – what kind of beautiful?*

Touch – *feel under fingertips, soles of feet, bottom; hot/cold, rough/smooth; things that touch you (breeze, raindrops, rim of glass); things you touch (yak's coat, palm trunk, kelim rug).*

Kinetic – *body position: awkward, comfy, stretched, cramped, turned, straight...*

Inner/visceral – *body organs, gut reactions: churning stomach, tight throat, full bladder, scratchy eyes, prickling scalp, gooseflesh, genitals responding (or not)*

Time – *night/day, evening; light, shadow (Monet's cathedral); time creeps, time whizzes*

Bubble-and-Riff, Listing, Serendipity Bag, Postcards, Sweetie Jar, Word Box: you can link the emphasis on senses with any of the stimulus exercises, and more. Some specific sense exercises follow here. Remind students of the senses often and praise good examples in their writing as frequently as possible.

10 EXERCISE: Travel and the Senses

List five places you have been on your travels and holidays. Choose one, bubble, write a paragraph that puts us there. This can lead to a travel article or fiction scene.

11 EXERCISE: Picture Senses

Provide suitable pictures (See **Postcards & Pictures,** ahead). *Choose or imagine a person in the scene; describe the sounds, smells and other sense-sensations they are experiencing in the setting.*

12 EXERCISE: Hyper-Awareness (surprise)

After introducing **8 Senses,** before a break (coffee or lunch) instruct students to be hyper-aware. On return to class, give one of these writing exercises.

- **Sheer observation** *Bubble and write, describing the canteen break, using as many of the senses as richly as possible.*

- **Character-based in two stages. Tutor, don't reveal the second stage till the first is written. Stage 1.** *Describe the canteen break as seen by a character who has just had a row with a lover – a paragraph or half-page.* **Stage 2.** *Same break, same character, but he/she has just declared love and learned it was mutual. Describe the break experience.*

13 EXERCISE: Hyper-Awareness (prepared variation)

After introducing **8 Senses,** before a break, instruct students to be hyper-aware under one of these conditions. Then students come back to write:

- **Inhabit the Child** *Imagine you are 4 - 5 years old, what do you see, notice, experience on the visit to the canteen?*

- **Focus** Distribute taskslips unique to each student, each with a single sense, or even a single colour or object *(hands, shoes, noses, blue, orange...)* to be acutely aware of, and come back and write about.

II. 25 Further Sparking Exercises

14 EXERCISE: Serendipity Bag

Here's a special treat, either to wow students early on, or to wake you all up in late-course doldrums. It requires some serendipitous advance work by the tutor.

Preparation. Find a basket, box or drawstring bag, the more mysterious or interesting-looking the better. Then the *objets trouvés* – found objects. Collect a range of odd items from around your life to put in it – and I do mean odd: that broken cracker puzzle, an old postmarked envelope, a pretty pocket mirror you never use, a scrap of ribbon, that funky key ring, a strange little bottle, a small teddy bear, a marble, a string of beads, an empty tape dispenser... be sure to have more than the number of students, in case someone finds an item totally impossible (which should not be allowed, technically, because the direction to such a student then is: *write about why you cannot write from this object*).

Exercise. Each student plunges hand in and takes whatever comes – it's best not to allow pre-meditation. Then off they go, bubbling and writing a paragraph or a page, letting the item remind, inspire, take them wherever it goes.

15 EXERCISE: Whose Is It? Serendipity Bag variation

Instead of freewheeling, you can focus the **Serendipity Bag** objects on character. *Describe the person who owned or owns this object, how did it come into their possession? What does it mean to them?*

16 EXERCISE: Alien View Serendipity Bag variation

How would a Martian or a foreigner or a child see this object? What would they imagine it is, does, could mean? Perhaps in their world it means something entirely other to our world?

17 EXERCISE: Blindman's Bluff Serendipity Bag variation

Ask students the week before to bring a scarf to class next time; some will forget, so bring some spares of your own. *In pairs, one of you blindfold yourself with a scarf. The other draws an object from the bag, and gives it to her or his partner who has to – by feel alone – guess what is. The guesser should describe all sensations and possibilities that occur, partner make notes of these.* When all is revealed they swap roles, drawing out a different object. Students can then write about the experience, or just talk about it, taking away with them the heightened sensory awareness and unusual angles that sense deprivation provides.

18 EXERCISE: Who's Desperate and Why?

This is a quickie using one object – could be something from the **Serendipity Bag** or any item that comes to hand as you need it: a newspaper, a pen, a handbag, a book…

Hold up or point out the item, and ask the class, writing individually as an exercise in 10 – 15 minutes, to describe why someone desperately wants or needs the item. They can describe the character and the scenario as well, in order to explain the motive. With further work this might turn into a short story.

19 EXERCISE: Stone Writing

Preparation. Rather like serendipity objects, but this time you make a trip to the gem shop. Collect a small boxful of semi-precious stones in their wondrous variety of colours, textures and patterns. You can add stripey, sparkly or textured stones picked up at the seashore and rocky streams. Or run a variation on this, using seashells. Find a good container, say of rattan or woven grasses for an elemental feel, or of velvet or lacquer, associating with valuable treasures.

Proffer the container letting students choose one of nature's objects, then contemplate, bubble and write whatever comes to mind. This usually brings excellent freewheeling results, but some other time you can prompt them if you wish, for instance:

- *Where has this been?*
- *What does your stone remind you of?*
- *Who found, or who treasures this natural item, and why?*
- *If it could talk (or if it had a smell, or if it was once a person)*

20 EXERCISE: Word Box

Preparation. Advance work for you again, as with **Serendipity Bag** and **Stone Writing**. Don't feel overburdened by all this preparation, once created these materials will support you for years of teaching. Your **Word Box** is a metal pencil case, say, or other small colourful or intriguing box. Have fun finding something that pleases you. Fill it with scores of words, even a hundred or more, typed and cut up into individual little taskslips. Offer the box, students choose one slip and, using the word on it, they **Bubble-and-riff** as explained earlier.

Word Box

Additives	Genome	Naked eye	Tiaras
Adultery	Gorilla	Neighbours	Telephones
Anoraks	Guarantees	Newfangled	
Aspirin		News headlines	
Aura	Handicrafts	Nursing	Umbrellas
	Harvests		Ultra-sound
Ballerinas	Hijacking	Obsessions	Underachievers
Batting	Housing	Oak	Unicorn
Beds	Hygiene	Obesity	University
Budgerigars		Oceans	
Buffalo	Icebergs	Olympics	Vampires
	Icon		Vasectomy
Cable	In-laws	Parachuting	Vegetables
Calories	Insomnia	Parties	Veteran's Day
Camping	Internet	Perfumes	Virus
Communications		Photography	
Creche	Jacket	Privacy	Waiters
	Jams		Walking
Decentralisation	Jargon	Quango	Watershed
Decanter	Jewellery	Quash	Weapons
Design	Judgment	Queen	Workaholic
Diplomas		Quotes	
Drugs	Karate		X-chromosome
	Kennels	Rainbows	Xmas
Eagle	Ketchup	Rapid eye movement	X-ray
Eating disorder	Killjoy	Regeneration	Xylophone
Education	Knapsacks	Rights	
Environment		Rubbish	Yahoo
Exclusive	Labels		Yarn
	Landlords	Safety	Year-end
Fashion	Laser	Sandwiches	Yoga
Fax	Licence	Saxophone	
Financial advice	Liquor	Siblings	
Flamenco		Sports	Zebra
Flooding	Malpractice		Zeus
	Mascots	Tankers	Zip
Gardening	Massage	Taxidermy	Zoom lens
Gemmology	Medals	Theft	Zucchini
	Monarchy		

21 EXERCISE: Sweetie Jar

Preparation. Similar to **Word Box,** but this time find a large penny-candy jar or cook's storage jar. Fill it with typed, cut-up individual taskslips, folded once or twice so they all fluff up like shredded paper or fortune-cookie fortunes (more fun if you print out your lists on various coloured paper). Lists to type and cut up:

- **Words,** as above, for short stimulus writing (5 - 10 minutes). The two below would need longer (10 - 20 minutes), and could lead to developing and finishing as rounded pieces or stories..

- **Wisdoms & Warnings** I collected these by getting the students to group-brainstorm sayings, both traditional and family or regionally eccentric. You can add extras of your own. Drawn from the jar, the exercise is then to write a story, memory or response that the saying triggers. A few examples:

    – You'd make a better door than you would a window..

    – (What shall I wear?) A bright blue ribbon and a rose in your hair.

    – Cat got your tongue?

    – Penny for your thoughts.

    – Don't cross your eyes, if the wind changes you'll stay that way forever.

    – Eat this! It'll put hairs on your chest!

    – A stitch in time saves nine.

    – (If you shiver) Someone just walked over your grave.

    – If you don't brush your hair bats will nest in it.

    – If you suck your thumb the scissor man will cut it off.

    – It will rain if you cry on your birthday.

    – If at first you don't succeed, give up!

    – I was at the airport when my ship came in.

    – Many mickle makes a muckle.

    – All fur coat and no knickers.

- **Story Prompt** I list some here, inspired by the 786 in Jason Rekulak's The Writer's Block.

  – Your first kiss – who, when, where, how did it feel?

  – Write a story about the images on a digital camera, using captions of not more than five sentences.

  – A speed-date session goes badly, despite the fact that your character deeply likes the other person.

  – Breakfast: write an argument between two characters.

  – Imagine that you could wake up tomorrow in someone else's powerful job. Whose? What are some of the first things you'd do?

  – Invent or describe a time you sneaked and read someone's post. What did it reveal to you about the person? How did you feel about yourself?

  – A forgery is discovered at a museum. Write about it.

  – Write a story set in the toilets of a gourmet restaurant.

  – Describe an embarrassing gift. What did the gift reveal about the giver?

  – Describe the first pet you ever had, and how it felt to touch – or the one you wanted but were never allowed to have.

22 EXERCISE: I remember...

Preparation. Less advance work than the **Sweetie Jar,** but similarly full of words and phrases. To be used over many sessions. Give out as a whole list to each student on a single sheet of paper (again, coloured paper adds to the creative feeling). Each week students choose a word and write for 10 - 15 minutes. You could plan this for 4-6 weeks, a regular slot, or just use it now-and-then over a longish course. One of my lists that bears fruit:

WORDSTARTS

Choose one of the following words/phrases and use it as a springboard to write. Any direction or interpretation you like. Save this list; we will use it in future classes.

I remember	Good morning
Thousands	Soil
Ice	Getting there
Looking back	Watching
The bridge	Bulge
Every so often	Next
Don't	Teaspoon
Nails	Friday
Mist	Aroma
Song	Slipper
Green	On the other hand

What's the point? Students might read out each week – they'll be interested in the variety of choices and responses. Or students can simply save up their writings, using the **'I remember'** series to build their portfolio of free creative writing. If you want to make more of it, at the end of the series have students select, say, three they judge best – thus practising self-criticism – to polish and submit as finished work.

23 EXERCISE: Writing from the Negative Wordstart variation

When they've written from the I remember list over a few weeks, make students contemplate the words they have NOT chosen. They must now write from one of these – what they don't like about the subject. There's wonderful power in antipathy.

EXERCISE METHOD: Postcards & Pictures

This requires the kind of **preparation** that becomes a lifetime hobby. Who can resist buying wonderful postcards at galleries and museums? You can cut fascinating photos out of magazines, too; The National Geographic's a good source, as are some Sunday supplements. (Usually it's best to glue these onto index cards for ease of handling.) Start collecting now and go on and on. I have several categories, not to say that they don't cross over sometimes. How to use them? There are many possibilities, some workable with almost any picture, others suitable to certain categories of cards. First, variations in distribution.

EXERCISE METHOD: Imperative Postcard

Distribute the postcards and instruct students to (bubble and) write the exercise.

EXERCISE METHOD: Chosen Postcard

Lay out a generous selection and let students choose a card that calls to them.

EXERCISE METHOD: Ambush Postcard

Part way through a given writing exercise (possibly even using another postcard as the stimulus) go round and drop a postcard at each student's place – they now have to swerve to incorporate something from this picture. This is particularly provocative if they are writing a story, monologue or riff.

24 EXERCISE: Postcards of Places

Travel postcards of streets, landscapes, buildings, foreign scenes; atmospheric photos; also postcards of paintings of land, sea or interiors. *Someone has just walked through/been in this place, who is it? Where was he/she coming from, going to? Why? What's on his or her mind?*

25 EXERCISE: Surreal Postcards

Strange abstracts; angled photos of weird items; mysterious, surreal, bizarre, funky or otherwise odd paintings or photos. *States of Heart – this picture represents someone's feelings and thoughts, write an interior monologue.*

26 EXERCISE: Situation Pictures

People doing things, the more puzzling or busy the better. *What's going on in this picture? Who are these people, why and what are they doing? OR Choose one person in the picture and write his or her thoughts, feelings, dialogue. OR Write the story of this situation.*

27 EXERCISE: Portraits

Painted or photographed. *Describe this person's life.* (Also see **Character** in *Craft* section.)

28 EXERCISE: Mythical Pictures

Fairytales, myths, legends, Bible tales, saints, heroes. *Write one scene of the story, as vividly as you can. OR Write a scene of this story that is unknown to the rest of the world. OR Write the thoughts and feelings of a person in this story.*

29 EXERCISE: Season and Element Pictures

Nature; close focus on rocks, water etc. *Put a character in this place/experience, why is he/she there, what thoughts, feelings and senses? OR Explain this to a child who has never seen it.*

30 EXERCISE: Animal Pictures

Especially wild animals in the outdoors. *You are a photographer or a scientist observing this animal, but at the same time it is reminding you of somebody else; write the train of thoughts.*

31 EXERCISE: Writing with the Senses

The **8 Senses** exercise (see earlier) works well with any of the above postcards and pictures. *Describe the smells, sounds, textures, movements in this picture.*

32 EXERCISE: Line from a Poem

Introduce to the class a rich, strong published poem from a class text or in a typed handout. After reading out and discussion of the poem's content, form and language, invite students to each choose one line that particularly draws them, and then to bubble and write from this line. The result can be a riff or a rough poem.

33 EXERCISE: Grab-Bag Line from a Poem variation

Choose a vividly imaged poem as above, but DO NOT show or discuss it in advance, thus keeping the stimulus completely fresh and uninfluenced. **Preparation:** type and cut into individual lines (multiple copies if needed). Students draw a strip at random, and write as above. After all the reading out present the originating poem.

What about plagiarism? Don't bring up this subject until after the **Line from a Poem** exercises, as its ramifications and discussion will only sidetrack and inhibit the freedom to write. As tutor, always credit the poem and the poet in due course. Some students will springboard from the line, only using a single word, image or thought from it, so plagiarism will not be an issue. Others might borrow the line in full; in this case once they have written they should eliminate that first borrowed line; it's remarkable how the new piece will stand on its own. If the piece absolutely needs to keep the original line, and the student intends to work further on the piece and send it out into the world, then the student should add a note to credit and thank the original inspiring poet.

34 EXERCISE: Writing by Prompts

Poet Kate Clanchy introduced me to this method at a Millennium workshop using historical materials at the Public Records Office. An imagination-releasing exercise, it provides a staged way in to the deeper writing trance, so allow more time than for a 'quickie' stimulus like **Word Box** or **Listing**. To **prepare,** select postcards or pictures with a number of people in them (see **Exercise 26: Situation Pictures**). If you can't find enough you can photocopy them, as each writer will respond uniquely to identical pictures. Contemplate the pictures and devise a series of open yet specific prompts which will lead students into creative exploration.

In class, distribute the pictures, allow a few moments study then ask the first question and allow a good 3 or so minutes for writing response. Then move on to the next prompt, as many as ten in all. Finally, allow 20 minutes minimum (an hour can feel too little!) for students to pull this material into a rough poem, story or riff. The prompts will vary depending on the pictures, but here are some examples:

– *Choose a central person in the picture, write how she or he sees what's going on here; use the first person: 'I, me, my'*

– *What is a smell in the picture? Describe it.* (After a moment:) *Describe another smell.*

– *What is the central person feeling?*

– *Write about the darkest part of the picture.*

– *What are the sounds in the scene? Describe the qualities of the sounds.*

– *What is this central person wearing, the texture, colour? How does he or she feel about it?*

– *Find the brightest part of the picture. Write about it.*

– *What is someone else in the scene thinking and feeling?*

– *Something is about to happen, what?*

35 EXERCISE: Propless Writing by Prompts

You can do a similar staged exercise without any pictures or props at all, just sheer creativity… it might even lead to a story. This comes from Deena Metzger's book Writing for Your Life:

- *List three nouns, like knife, egg, moon.* [1 minute]
- *Describe a landscape that has the following qualifications: you yourself have never actually been on this landscape. At the moment you are describing it, no people are on it.* [7 minutes]
- *A character appears on the landscape, a character you have never written or thought about. Describe the character.* [7 minutes]
- *Now finally, add an action. This action must include the three nouns you listed. Combine the landscape, the character, the nouns into an action.* [15 minutes]

36 EXERCISE: The Rant

This is a short, energy-filled exercise that requires absolutely no preparation on your part. Have students list (see **Listing** exercises, earlier) *five pet peeves,* things that really bug them, like *people who litter, marketing phone calls* etc. Or have them list *household chores you loathe.* Then direct students to choose one, and let rip in a type of **Chaos Writing** (see **Toolkit 2**) rant. Encourage them to be as wild and exaggerated as they like. If you wish, start them off: *I can't stand people who… OR I really hate it when…*

What's the point? This is great fun for letting off steam, good for laughter in class. There's a lot of power in the negative; this could also be the basis for a character who goes to extremes.

37 EXERCISE: Peer Imperative

There is something undeniably compelling about being given a stimulus by the tutor, of course, but all the more so by this exercise. Prepare, or have students tear from their notebooks, a half sheet of paper. Each student writes one word on the paper – an object, something touchable. All then crumple this piece of paper and toss it to the middle of the room (assuming the class is arranged in a U-shape); then all get up and pick up one of the 'gifts'. Open the paper, sit, bubble and write from the word.

Obviously this one can be a lifesaver if you're caught short with extra class time! Also, you can use it to inject a fresh note to class; there's something very freeing about that crumpling up, and about drawing on each others' word store and imperative. **Alternatives:** instead of crumpling, instruct them to fold the papers; instead of tossing down, collect the papers in a bag, box, bin or large envelope. **Multiple variation:** Write two different words on two different pieces of paper; after mixing them all up each person chooses two and writes, incorporating both words. Try it with three!

38 EXERCISE: Peer Imperative Character variation

Similar to the above, write a first name on the paper. On a second piece of paper write an age. Keep each pile separate; people draw one from each pile, and from name and age alone, write a monologue by this character, or a description of the character and his/her problem.

39 EXERCISE: Reflective Writing

Here's an inward-facing exercise, and one that requires no preparation by the tutor. Towards the end of a session, or after a lively discussion or exercise, say: *Take 5 minutes to write to yourself, sum up and absorb, reflecting on what we've just been doing, what you've gained from it, how it affects you. This will be just for yourselves, not to read out.*

What's the point? To breathe and allow the student to consolidate the experience relevant to his/her own self and writing.

III. PAIRING DEVICES & EXERCISES

Pairing exercises are useful throughout a course. Of course you can simply ask students to turn to a neighbour and begin a task; for a one-day course this is the most efficient method for introductions and paired exercises, and for many exercises over a longer course you'll also pair as neighbours to save time and babble. But a creative class should be lively, rousing people from ruts of thinking, being and writing, so as well as pairing to introduce people, try some of these when you want a warm, fun lift to the atmosphere.

The task might be **Mini-interviews,** to report back to the group as introductions for a first session (see *Nurture* section). Or you can use the exercises below as introductory tasks, or as stimulus exercises in their own right.

40 EXERCISE: Word-match

Excellent for warming a group; prepare a duplicate set of index cards, writing a single word on each card. Choose interesting yet common experience words like: chocolate, starting school, driving, moving house, dentist, birthplace, waking up, holiday (last), holiday (next), exercise. **Instructions:** *Find your match-card partner and tell each other an association with or an experience of the word.* The chatting may be all there is to the exercise, or it can lead to general introductions or individual writing on the subject.

Variations: think up two positive and two negative aspects of the word; brainstorm a story from the word.

41 EXERCISE: Picture-match

As word-match, but use matching postcards (from travels or museums), or paste magazine photos on index cards, then cut in half. Tasks: along the lines of word-match, and see **Postcards & Pictures** in *Stimulus* section.

42 EXERCISE: Quiz-match

Depending on how knowledgeable the group is, you can prepare a set of index cards half of which have, say, the name of an author, the other half a book title by the author. *Jane Austen/Pride and Prejudice, Ian McEwan/Enduring Love, Joseph Heller/Catch-22* etc However, not all wannabe writers are readers, sad to say, so this might deflate confidence: not your goal. Get to know the class first.

43 EXERCISE: Quote-match

Type, cut out and paste on index cards or simply cut in strips, quotes from writers on writing. **Variations:** famous quotes; proverbs or sayings. *Find the person who has the same quote you've been given.* Task ideas: agree or disagree with quote (three reasons why), reinvent quote, what did the speaker's spouse say, brainstorm a story...

GENERAL GUIDELINES FOR ALL PAIRING EXERCISES

- Keep the pair devices in two separate identical sets to give out on opposite sides of the room, doing a quick count to check your numbers, so that your distribution will get people moving and mixing as they search for their match.

- Be sure to explain the task BEFORE they rise – you'll never be able to shout over the noise once the happy chatter begins.

- Stroll about, dropping the match-cards randomly at people's places. As they find each other, write task-point reminders on the board – some students do not fully heed or remember verbal instructions.

- Watch the clock. Allow about10 minutes for the paired task. Give a countdown at two minutes, then one minute, reminding pairs to cover the task points.

- What if your numbers are uneven? For odd numbers, you, as tutor, can join in and become half of a pair. However, you need to write those task reminders on the board and be timekeeper, so I prefer to designate one pair as a threesome, and make a third-match card for this purpose. This is also a solution for the late-arriving student. The trio simply have to make do with the time allotted.

- When time's up the pairs report on the task to the group at large. Or you may have them write for 5 - 10 minutes as an individual exercise, if that was the task. I have students return to original seats for the whole-group work, so partners may be across the room, not adjacent – it's less routine, sharpens attention.

IV. END-OF-COURSE FUN AND GAMES

As the holiday season approaches, or at the end of a course, students usually moot a party. If they don't suggest one yourself! Institutions usually allow the bringing in of crisps and beverages… guide students to organising that. For entertainment, choose one of these party games for creative people. They're done in stages; each player needs pen and a sheet of paper which must be folded down to conceal what's written before being passed to the next player. The passing along and keeping up usually goes awry – all part of the fun.

44 EXERCISE: A Story of Consequences

Stage 1. *All write the name of a male famous person at the top of the page. Alive or dead, ancient or modern, fictional, from myth or current affairs…Fold over to conceal this, and pass to the left.*

Stage 2. *All write the word AND, and then the name of a female famous person; same wide-ranging options. Fold over, pass to the left.*

Stage 3. *Now write 'MET AT…' and write the place where 'they' met. If you prefer you can say 'met in' or 'met under', as in 'Met at heaven's gate' or 'Met under the Eiffel Tower.' Fold over, pass left.*

Stage 4. *Write 'HE SAID:' and whatever a he might say. A quippy comment, an innuendo, a chat-up line, a bold statement… Fold over and pass.*

Stage 5. *Write 'SHE SAID:' and whatever a she might say. Fold over and pass.*

Stage 6. *Now write 'AND THEN THEY…' and whatever a he and a she might then do to end the story.*

Read out one by one and enjoy the fun.

45 EXERCISE: Unseen Questions & Answers

Stage 1. *All write a riddle-type or quiz-type question at the top of their sheet of paper. They can be quirky, existential, fantastical, political, childlike... (Do you know why the dog howls at the moon? Is time shrinking? Will creative writing classes survive?) Fold over and write the letter A: (for answer) in the next space, and pass to the left.*

Tutor, you need to tell students to write in the letters Q and A as prompts to help sort out the hopeless and hilarious muddles these exercises in rounds are prone to.

Stage 2. *Now, without looking at the hidden question, write an answer. It can be a brief statement of fact, a bit of wisdom or naughtiness, advice, instructions, fantastical... (Stags lose their antlers. Tie a knot in it. When it rains up instead of down...) Fold over and write the letter Q: in the next space, and pass to the left.*

Stage 3. *As the first round, write a question, fold over, write letter A and pass on.*

Stage 4. *As the second round, write an answer, fold over, write letter Q and pass on.*

Rounds 5-6. *Continue as above. Six-eight rounds is about enough.*

Reading out. In turn, all read out these surreal, delightful and often astoundingly synchronistic creations.

Section 3

CRAFT: Producing the work

    I. Story
    II. Character
    III. Point of View
    IV. Dialogue
    V. Scene & Plot
    VI. Storytelling Devices
    VII. Deeper into Character
    VIII. Richer Writing
    IX. Dip into Poetry
    X. Fixing a Story

Section 3
CRAFT: Producing the Work

People, especially beginners, love to play at the fun of writing, the *Stimulus* of the previous section. But real writers produced finished work, with a spark of inspiration at the start (their own or from class), development over hours, days, weeks or years, and polishing at the end. Crafting is the long middle part. If it helps your students, liken writing craft to learning to dance, or to making a chair – the beautiful idea is not enough, they have to get to grips with doing if they want a honed skill and a finished product.

Most areas of crafting make a mini-series over several sessions with a variety of exercises to provide hands-on experience for your students. For short, concentrated courses you can use just one exercise for each craft focus. Keep the pace lively: dialogue, character, point of view or whatever, I advise you to plunge in with an exercise first. Backup afterwards with mini-lectures, analysis of good writing examples and how-to handouts. Too much explanation at the start will only inhibit your writers.

Plan more time for these exercises (30 - 40 minutes) than for *Stimulus* bursts. Structure the briefing, the writing time, then reading out and feedback (See **Writing and Reading Out,** in *Nurture),* then possibly further information. You may want to schedule the coffee break after writing, before reading.

A lot of these exercises function as stimuli which may lead to longer, developed work by students – great! I always encourage that, but the main point is to give students craft practice in the classroom towards their own work later on.

Note: this section addresses prose fiction – short story and novel. Much is applicable or adaptable for teaching memoir (life-writing), plays and narrative poetry.

MINI-LECTURE 3: Elements of Fiction

This is the briefest of highlights for a quick lecture as you launch into story-writing, to be followed with **Rainbow Tales, Plunge into Action** or one of the deeper exercises in the *Stimulus* section. Put the key points on a transparency or disc for projection or else just write on the whiteboard, a focus as you talk it through.

ELEMENTS OF STORY

Character(s)	needs, desires = motivation
Plot	something has to happen action, forward movement
Conflict/struggle	obstacle(s) to character's need/desire character + obstacle = plot, the story
Setting	time, place, atmosphere
Point of view	who tells the story
Theme	mood or core of story, what it's 'about' often unstated; may emerge as you write

My favourite illustration as I talk through the points: *Say you have a man who gets up, goes to the park, comes home, has dinner, goes to sleep. NO STORY: the character is satisfied with his life and nothing of interest happens. BUT if he...* and then sketch in an incident in the park with a dog, for instance, or a hooligan, and/or a character situation: he is out of money, he is lonely etc...

Instead, or as well, you might make brief references to a currently widely known film, TV drama or book. Be brief, don't talk at them: skip the academics, get down to writing.

I. STORY EXERCISES

46 EXERCISE: Rainbow Tales

There is something compelling about being given clues and told to go on and make a story from them, something… magic. We humans have a natural need to pattern, especially those with a creative urge. Even timid beginning writers respond to this exercise with satisfaction, often with chuckles of delight at how readily the story delivers itself. Allow a good 40 minutes: 5 minutes to brief and settle, 15-20 minutes to write in class, the rest to read out. Of course the pieces will need further work to become complete short stories.

Preparation. Use five different colours of paper or card, cut into pieces, say 5 x 2 inches (12 x 5 cm). This exercise, amplified from Joan Downar's exercise Coloured Runes in the Taking Reality by Surprise collection, is visually pleasing and illustrates the elements of story. Choose one colour each for: A character. Situation. Setting. Time. Theme. Print each cue card with a word or phrase from the appropriate category (lists below). Keep them sorted together into colours. I've used **Rainbow Tales** for years, and every time I'm amazed, as are students, at how well five random elements fall naturally into a story.

Explain the elements (below) – you might even choose one of each at random from your 'deck' and demonstrate on the board as you explain, getting students to pitch in with bubble ideas. Then walk round the room distributing five colours to each student. It's fun to splay out the deck (words unseen) and let people choose their own, magician style. Then they settle to write – beg them NOT to write on the coloured cards, to save you re-making. Remind them to bubble first.

A character *Remember that one character leads to others; you may find your story becomes more focussed on a character linked to the one you're given – that's okay.*

>   A violin teacher   An alcoholic
>   A gap year student   A confirmed bachelor
>   A newly wed man   A widow
>   An athlete   A doctor

49

A shopkeeper
A travel courier
A ten-year-old

A runaway
A mother of twins
A rock star

Situation *This could be the start or the middle or even the ending of the story, whatever works.*

An escape
New clothes
Redundant
Exams
A car crash
Lost
Bomb scare

A birth
Captured
A sleepless night
A discovery
An argument
Something is missing
A reunion

Setting *This setting might be at the start or later, and you might have several other settings as well.*

Heathrow Airport
A forest
A queue
Backstage
A classroom
Leisure centre
A gallery

Sauna
Bedroom
Airplane
Theme park/fun fair
Playground
Small village
A nursery

Time *The time you're given can be one of the trickiest – if it doesn't work with the ideas that are forming, don't worry about it. On the other hand, don't forget that characters can remember back to a time, imagine forward or dream of a time, as well as be IN a time.*

Spring
Evening
Winter
Lunchtime
New Year's Eve
Morning
Midnight

Yesterday
6 pm
2 years back
1945
1918
2 generations back
Anniversary

Theme *Theme can throw you off into a moralistic little lesson instead of storytelling, so ignore this if you like. But it might give you ideas for motives or ending.*

There's always tomorrow	Owning up
If only	Regret
Evil	Love
Freedom	Envy
Be true to yourself	Live for the moment
Truth will out	Loneliness
Revenge	Bitterness

47 EXERCISE: Stone Soup

Once I forgot to bring my Rainbow cue cards – it made a good lesson to have the students provide the cues themselves, like the folk tale about the village that had no food to offer the stranger, but ended up with a hearty soup thanks to his devices. It's like **Peer Imperative** in *Stimulus,* but more complex. Donating quarter- or eighth-page pieces of paper, first each student writes one **character type and age** *(say, makeup-artist, 30).* Next, on a separate piece of paper, students write a **situation** *(say, moving house),* and so on including **setting, time** and **theme**. Collect each round as you go; be careful to keep the piles separate. When complete, each student draws from each pile, and with the five elements they're off to writing, as with **Rainbow Tales** above.

48 EXERCISE: Plunge into Action

Adapted from an exercise on the BBC Get Writing website, this 'elements of story' exercise uses the patterning creative urge and has produced a surprising number of completed short stories. Why? Probably the two elements of motive and specific action. You can present the exercise as a crime story, for that's what the actions are – but for those who shy away from murder and mayhem (like me), remind students that the actions can be interpreted variously. *Shoot* might be shooting a rubber band at someone; *drown* or *torch* might be the destruction of a prized or symbolic possession, and so on.

As with **Rainbow Tales** you need to **prepare** cards or task slips in advance, and have students draw one from each pile. Again, use different coloured papers to help you keep track of the four elements.

Protagonist AND Victim Do these in duplicate, in two different colours. Repetition doesn't matter, you can even include duplicates within each pile if you need to make up the numbers, as the ingenious end results will prove! *Tell students: Draw one from Protagonist (or Perpetrator) pile, and one from Victim pile.*

farmer	banker
child	tourist
jilted lover	stripper
neighbour	motorist
birdwatcher	builder
bride	priest

Motive *Draw just one of these – the protagonist's reason for acting upon the victim.*

greed	excitement
attention	ambition
desire	boredom
jealousy	anger
fear	pride
grief	envy
shame	lust
paranoia	laziness

Action *Draw one of these, the act the protagonist inflicts upon the victim. Remember, if you are not comfortable with crime you can soften the action, or the protagonist might fail at the final point.*

steals	knifes
torches	strangles
kidnaps	smothers
mugs	drowns
poisons	assaults
shoots	runs over

> **TIP: How long is a short story? How long is a novel?**
> Students will ask. I tell them the usual short story competition word limits (1000, 1,500, 2,500, 4,000), and point out the range from mini twist-in-the-tale stories in mass market weekly magazines to 5-9,000 word literary stories which are very hard to find markets for. EM Forster says 70,000 words is the minimum for a novel; 55,000 is the typical Mills & Boon genre romance or Dick Francis crime story; 35,000 can make a juvenile novel; 100,000 is what many mainstream publishers want, to a maximum of 120,000; some sagas reach 200-300,000 words. If you want to turn this into lesson content see **Reading for Writers** *(Running the Course)*, **Finding a Publisher or Agent** *(Process)*, **Adjectives/Adverbs** *(Craft)*.
>
> Your main point: writing short stories is an excellent way to develop craft. One famous author said aspirers should write fifty short stories before embarking on a novel – that always gets gasps from students!

II. CHARACTER EXERCISES

After your **Elements of Story** mini-lecture you might want to go directly to character, as it is a rich way in to story-writing. Then you could use the **Story Exercises** above later in the course. You can make an entire 2-hour class of the **Character Profile** exercise below with its extensions, or indeed carry the extensions through several sessions and on into a full short story.

Throughout the character exercises pick out and praise points that contribute generally to good story writing – say, *a sibling or friend is useful as a confidante for the character.* Or, *the classic tragic flaw is when a strong attribute taken to extreme becomes a weakness – ambition, for instance, or generosity.* This kind of 'as and when' guidance is much more lively than a straightforward lecture; you can always sum up on the whiteboard or in a handout if you worry about missing out points.

49 EXERCISE: Character Profile

I regard this as essential to teaching fiction writing. **Preparation:** save up magazines – I find Sunday supplements the best source – and clip out a whole gallery of characters. Choose interesting faces and a range of ages; models in advertisements and women's magazines don't look real enough: cliché faces inspire cliché characterisation. I prefer photographs to painted portraits (see **Postcards & Pictures** in *Stimulus* section) for a feeling of reality. Build up your collection over time. Stick each cutout on a 5 x 7 inch unlined index card, an equal number of males and females.

Type and photocopy the character profile below as a full page worksheet. Hand out worksheet and give one character picture to each student, offering them only choice of gender. Instructions: *Study the picture for a little while, then complete the character profile. Then we will introduce our characters to the class.*

CHARACTER PROFILE

1. NAME:
2. AGE:
3. STATURE/BUILD:
4. COLOUR/STYLE HAIR:
5. COLOUR EYES:
6. EDUCATIONAL BACKGROUND:
7. WORK EXPERIENCE:
8. BEST FRIEND:
9. PARTNER (IF ANY):
10. ENEMIES AND WHY:
11. PARENTS/SIBLINGS/CHILDREN:
12. HOBBY/PASTIME/PLEASURES:
13. FAVOURITE MUSIC/COLOURS
14. PRESENT PROBLEMS:
15. STRONGEST & WEAKEST CHARACTER TRAITS:

Allow a good 15 minutes on the profile worksheet. When ready, call on each student in turn to hold up the picture and to introduce the character to the class, going through the whole profile. By questions 6-15 these new characters come alive. As each student finishes his or her presentation, ask a further question for on-the-spot response. This demonstrates to the students that they do indeed KNOW from within rather than impose from above when they are delving in the creative sphere.

Spot Questions: How well do you know your character? Ask each student a different spot question, such as:
- *What is on your character's bedside table?*
- *Describe your character's living room.*
- *Does he/she own a car? If not, what kind of transport is used? If yes, what kind and colour car?*
- *What will your character eat for dinner tonight? OR last night?*
- *What will he/she wear tomorrow?*
- *Your character has a pet – what is it? Name?*
- *Your character just lost some money in a drinks vending machine. What was it? What does he or she do now?*
- *Your character has just received a job offer. What is it? He/she will not accept it, why?*

Then go on to ask the student, *How will the character's present problem get worse?* This is vital to get your writers thinking about obstacles and conflict that will drive a story forward. Some people will have fairly bland, un-problematic problems… tutor's job is to point out how these can be strengthened to make a stronger story.

50 EXERCISE: Monologues for Discovering a Character

Time now to write on this **Profile Character,** a monologue exercise to adapt as suits your teaching situation. You can have students follow on with it immediately in class or suggest they do it at home. Or they can do a monologue in class, and you can give a different one to do at home. Or you can use several monologues over several weeks in class. Ask for a half-page, maximum one page of writing. Some won't be sure what monologue means, so it helps to give a starting phrase, and to explain: *This is just the character thinking to himself, don't worry about setting, actions, dialogue or other characters. It's an interior monologue, as if he's lying awake in bed, as if she's daydreaming or talking to herself in her head.* Later you'll cover dialogue and action; the point here is to get deeper into a single character, and via the prompt to get into the

character's feelings, situation and relationships. Some examples:
- *Tomorrow's my birthday. I hope...*
- *I wish last weekend had turned out differently. I wanted...*
- *I hate this kind of rain. It always reminds me of...*
- *Each time he leaves I...*

After **reading out,** tell students to KEEP THESE MONOLOGUES because there are other uses for them in class. (See **Expanding Monologue** and **POV Exercises.**)

51 EXERCISE: Character Profile from a Name (variation)

A variation on magazine photographs to use with the **Character Profile** exercise is to provide a name and age. You can simply assign them, or you can have students draw taskslips from bags or piles – first names, last names, ages – for endlessly random combinations. It's remarkable how much a writer can KNOW from a name like *Esther Pasqual, 46,* or *Andrew Smithson-Johns, 30.* Proceed with the same spot questions and monologues.

52 EXERCISE: Expanding Monologues

One character leads to another, and might in fact make a better story than the first profile character. After students have written at least one monologue as above, have them write and read out a monologue by a person listed in the life of the character in the original profile:

- *the rival or opposition to the profile character*
- *possibly a supportive or witnessing character (parent, partner, friend, sibling)*

Tell students this monologue will illuminate the profile character, so the monologue might begin: *I couldn't believe it when NAME OF CHARACTER (that is, your first Profile character)* ...And the thoughts of the thinking character include:

- *What the profile character did that concerns the thinker*

- *What the character wears (clothes, accessories), appearance (hair; kempt, slobbish etc)*
- *How the character looks and sounds (voice, mannerisms, a phrase of dialogue)*

Deeper into Character. See further on in *Craft* for more character exercises.

III. POINT OF VIEW EXERCISES

In a one term or one year course it's time now to move on from story elements and character to more technical design choices of story-making: **Point of View (POV)** in both its senses. I've put **Story Point of View** and **Person Point of View** together here because the subjects come up in exercise discussions as story content overlaps into story tone. You might instead prefer to cover them separately. Verb use may arise and you could do exercises with **Tenses** here, too I've put some in **Richer Writing** (later in *Craft*).

53 EXERCISE: Agony Letter

For **Story Point of View**, I use the word *faceting* to explain the stage of considering a story idea and deciding *Whose story is it?* and *Who's telling the story?* Using small group work, this lively, staged exercise demonstrates the ways a story can develop, and it can be a *stimulus* into a full story if you wish.

Preparation. Comb women's magazines to find the Agony Aunt pages and read through the dilemmas presented, selecting 4 - 6 situations for class material. Search for mini-dramas that involve three or more people and are not too weird or painful. Copytype or clip and photocopy, leaving out the reply; you need multiple copies of each letter so that everyone in one small group of 3 - 4 students has a copy.

Pull the tables and chairs around so that four students can sit in each group – try to get to class early to do this, to save class time; besides, the surprise room rearrangement livens the class, providing a change of pace. Each group gets one Agony Letter, a copy for each student. If you're caught short it's fine for two groups to have the same letter, because the results are always different. If you're short of students the exercise will work with pairs.

Stage 1 (10-15 minutes). *Read and study the Agony Letter in your group. Then, together as a group, list the characters, decide on their names and ages. You can add any other characters if necessary, children or neighbors or boss, for instance. Also, agree any geographic locations and time-spans if relevant, for example, how long widowed or where they live.*

Discuss the story – what is happening and what could happen – as you do this.

Stage 2 (quickly). *Each person in the group now chooses one character in the story to write from – group agrees who's being whom, so there are no duplicates.*

Stage 3 (10-15 minutes). *Now, individually, write a first-person monologue as the character you've taken. How she or he feels about the situation, what their experience has been, what they think ... any aspect of the situation, any time in and around the situation. One-half to a full page.*

Stage 4 (20-30 minutes; probably best to go for break before this stage). *Now each group, one writer at a time, reads out to the whole class their pieces written from their character's point of view. DO NOT read out or tell the Agony Letter story, just read out all the characters' voices.*

As each group's reading progresses you'll have ample opportunities to draw attention to *Whose story is it?* and *Who's telling the story?*

Alternative Stage 3 (for more advanced class; 10-20 minutes). *Now, individually, write a scene from your character's point of view, opening with a line of dialogue. Include dialogue, action, setting. It can be in first person or third person.*

MINI-LECTURE 4:
Story Point of View & Person Point of View

The previous exercise, Agony Letter, tried out Story Point of View. Your story-makers needed to look for the viewpoint character to decide Whose story is it? Who's telling the story? Now they need to practice the other POV choice. Person Point of View delves into grammar, which may feel uncomfortable to some students, so keep to a short preface and a follow-up handout. Use brief, lively illustrative quotes from some of your own favourite authors. Begin with...

When faceting the viewpoint character for a story, keep the following in mind –

- *What do you want the reader to know?*
- *Who is in a position to be present during critical scenes?*
- *Who has a big stake in the outcome of the story? Who will be changed?*
- *Another important choice: what tone do you want your story to have? Reader's close involvement and caring about the character? Detached, ironic? Fragmented, many POVs? This leads to Person Point of View.*

I recommend inserting the **Transcribing POV** exercise here, then in discussion introduce the **Person Point of View** options (and handout) with their technical names, their advantages (or not) and good illustrations from published authors.

PERSON POINT OF VIEW

1) First person: I, me.
2) Second Person: You
3) Limited Third Person: He, She – one character's mind
4) Multiple Third Person: He, She – several characters' minds.
5) Omniscient Point of View – go into everybody's mind

54 EXERCISE: Transcribing POV

You can go on to a longer lecture and examples of **Person Point of View,** but I suggest some writing first, and the most natural exercise is to have students take a piece of their own first person monologue writing and transcribe it into third person. Choose from those above: **Agony Letter** or **Monologues for Discovering a Character.** Or start afresh with a **Life-Listing** exercise *(Stimulus)* section) and allow 5 - 10 minutes writing of a memory in first person.

Instructions. Whatever the starting point, tell students to transcribe their first person piece into third person – it's good to spring this instruction as a surprise, **before** the POV mini-lecture, so that they have written in first person without forethought. As they set about the task some will ask – and this is the point of the exercise – about other changes that the shift from first to third person requires. For now just tell them to make whatever changes they need to.

Read out. Don't have students read out until both first and third person versions are complete. Ask for general responses about how the exercise felt, then do a read-round; all the first person versions, then all the third, works well for illustrating and provoking discussion. Now's the time to point out differences in tone and the challenges in writing first vs third person point of view.

Variation. Copytype short passages of published fiction in various **Person Points of View** and photocopy as taskslips. Have students transcribe them: third to first, first to third, even second person into first or third, or the reverse.

IV DIALOGUE EXERCISES

Many students use dialogue right from the start, although many beginners err on the side of total narration. New or advanced, all writers can benefit by a focus on dialogue, either in one-off exercises or in a series of sessions. Dialogue follows well from **Elements of Story, Character** and **POV**, or you can let students carry on with dialogue instinctively and go instead to **Scene and Plot**, saving dialogue til later in the course. My whimsy is to alternate year to year.

55 EXERCISE: One-line Plunge

Don't freeze your students into self-consciousness with a dialogue lecture; start with an exercise. **Prepare** taskslips with single dialogue lines; students are to simply carry on writing the scene. Duplicates or even triplicates of the same starter-quote are fine, because no two students will invent the same follow-on. Select quotes that demand a response from another character to insure lively scenes. Allow 10-15 minutes and ask for a half-page or page of writing, reminding students that the emphasis is on the characters talking, but not to forget some sense of setting and action. Some ideas for quotes:

- *She grabbed me in the ladies' loo. 'Oh please like him, Sarah!' she squealed. She was high.*
- *'How do you feel about my offer to adopt you?' Rollo asked.*
- *Lysander and the woman stared at each other. In the pause a distant siren wailed. 'What did you do that for?' she said.*

The group **read-round** afterwards gives you the chance to comment on good dialogue points and missed opportunities, leading into general remarks.

MINI-LECTURE 5: Why Dialogue?

- *To bring a story or account to life, like a film or play, right before the reader's eyes*
- *To show, not tell, putting the reader into the scene as it happens*
- *To illuminate characters – what they say, how they say it, shows what the character is like (characterisation). Test: does this dialogue reveal or confirm something about the character?*
- *To move the story along – confrontation, evasion, information, innuendo... the dialogue isn't chit-chat, it's part of the story. Test: is this conversation going somewhere?*
- **(Later.** More dialogue exercises follow, so after a few, do a mini-lecture on any points that have not been covered naturally from students' work or questions, such as: 'said' is an invisible word, dialogue too real, dialogue not real enough, overuse of character names, script-like 'talking heads' with no sense of character or setting, over- and under-attribution, dialect and foreign languages. Another follow-up might focus on handling character's thoughts, which sometimes flummoxes students.)

56 EXERCISE: Surreal Dialogue

This is a silly escapade inspired by Gillian Allnutt and Barbara Trapido that puts the emphasis on characterisation through dialogue. **Prepare** a set of 20 cue cards, in two colours. Students pull one of each colour.

Red set: a ballet slipper, a red plastic bucket, an electric torch, a fountain pen, a clock radio, a teaspoon, a wool scarf, a set of car keys, a down-feather duvet, a television remote control

Yellow set: Stalin's moustache, Marilyn Monroe's bra, de Gaulle's hat, Marie Antoinette's wig, Cleopatra's sandal, Father Christmas's beard, Nelson's eyepatch, Picasso's striped T-shirt, the Queen's tiara, Queen Victoria's wedding ring

Instructions. *Write a dialogue between these two objects as if they were characters meeting for the first time, perhaps at a standup party or a dinner. Don't say what they are; only through the conversation as they get to know each other will the reader pick up hints. Don't worry about setting, but you can put in tone of voice and small actions. Do a half or one full page.*

Read-round afterwards, the exaggeration is great fun. See if everyone can guess the items, or at least some things about them.

57 EXERCISE: Dialogue Technicalities – Conventional

Blame the parlous state of grammar-teaching, or students' carelessness or rebellion against rules – dialogue punctuation and layout is only correctly done by about one in five creative writing students. Wordprocessing is a contributing factor, too, due to the prevalence of single-spaced block paragraphs (more on this in **Presentation** in *Process* section). You can tell, tell, tell students the rules to little avail – and you don't want to turn creative writing into a boring or scary school-days lesson. So finally I devised a way to make students see and understand the function and importance of dialogue conventions.

Preparation. Find a good dialogue scene in a published novel. (See **About using extracts in teaching** at the start of this book.). Look for one that has a good shape: narrative intro/beginning/set up, middle with dialogue that rises to some kind of climax, resolution and ending/fade out in narrative. Be sure it has setting and actions. You can use this scene again later for **Shape of a Scene** exercise. My favourite passage is from Maeve Binchy's The Lilac Bus. (Best to find your own favourite passage, but see *Sources* for the scene's page number if you need it.)

Copytype this scene, and then use your computer word programme to present it four different ways on four different sheets. Sheets 1, 3, 4 you can staple together and recycle for each course, using them as demo-samplers, not to be taken away. Sheet 2 is a worksheet.

Sheet 1. Double-spaced with NO PUNCTUATION MARKS, NO PARAGRAPHING. *After students puzzle over this for a bit, explain: Dense, isn't it? Here you see why we need paragraphs. They help the reader to understand and to flow through the story.*

Sheet 2. Double-spaced and laid out conventionally as it would be in manuscript sent to agent/editor, but PUNCTUATE ONLY FIRST TWO PARAGRAPHS. *This is dialogue and manuscript layout to normal conventions – it is how editors expect to see your work. It is punctuated at the start. Go on now and finish the page – notice that punctuation is INSIDE the quote mark. And a new paragraph starts for each change of speaker. This helps the reader understand the story without having to stop and think. You want FLOW, not snags and stumbles which take your reader out of the reading trance.*
When finished, have people compare their punctuating and discuss any issues that arise.

Sheet 3. Single-spaced, punctuated and laid-out correctly to conventions. *This is how it appeared in the book. But notice how hard it would be to make amendments; and how hard on the eyes 200 - 400 pages in manuscript would be. You must be kind to your editor.*

Sheet 4. Single-spaced with gaps between paragraphs, and paragraphs not indented. *This is word processor lay-out as we are used to seeing on screen and in business documents and leaflets – but GAP ON THE PAGE is NOT for fiction writing, not even for non-fiction. The gap creates leaps and hurdles for your readers. Again, you want the lulling easy flow of story, one paragraph leading the eye and mind into the next. Without gaps,* *you must indent to indicate new paragraphs. White space on the page signifies a change of scene or jump in time. If you are ever in doubt, look at the daily newspapers and at books; be aware of their use of layout.*

58 EXERCISE: Dialogue Technicalities – Non-conventional

To give normal dialogue punctuation and layout conventions a chance to sink in, I find it best to wait a session or two before offering cutting-edge styles of dialogue presentation – no quote marks. So, when you feel ready, copytype short passages from several different authors as a sampler handout. Irvine Welsh devised a system for Trainspotting, Michèle Roberts has her own style and so on. As well as discussing the impact, pros and cons, you could make this an exercise: have students write a dialogue scene conventionally (in this session or from a previous exercise), then re-write it in a non-conventional style, to see how it feels.

V. SCENE and PLOT EXERCISES

Now that your students have a bit of a grasp of character and dialogue, it's time to get those characters acting and reacting in a setting – it's time for scene. This makes a good mini-series; you could choose instead to introduce scene before the specifics of dialogue, possibly even before character. In **Shape of the Whole Story,** later, you'll get students building scenes into the dramatic tension of plot, but first the building block itself, the active scene. Of course your students were writing scenes in dialogue; this is a more structural approach.

MINI-LECTURE 6: What's a Scene?

Everybody instinctively knows what a scene is – just think of actors on a stage before your eyes, or think of film and TV dramas: characters we are interested in, in a single setting, a single length of time, talking, moving, interacting. There's one further element: tension. The scene has to be going somewhere. As we've said earlier about the elements of a whole story, it has to be about something. Two people chatting by the coffee machine – real? Yes, but who cares. Two people chatting by the coffee machine both after the same promotion... and one lies about his true intentions – aha, we perk up. Scene brings the situation alive for the reader. It slows down time to more-or-less actuality, so that the reader lives through the moment with the main character.

What's the opposite of scene? Narrative summary, which explains, describes, fills in or summarises. [Tutor: read out two brief passages from a work of your choice to illustrate scene v narrative.] *Narration is a necessary and important part of storytelling, but it does not bring the story alive. Prose of entirely narrative summary is muffled, unengaging. That's the reason for the phrase you may have heard: Show, don't tell.*

59 EXERCISE: Show, Don't Tell

After the mini-lecture, there's nothing like showing and doing to make the **Show, Don't Tell** point, so here's an exercise inspired by Barbara Seuling's How to Write a Children's Book and Get It Published. **Prepare** these two taskslips and divide equally between class members. You can just alternate around the room, or put students in small groups and give every student in one group the same slip; another group gets the other slip – be sure it's one per student, however, because this is an individual writing (actually re-writing) exercise.

Instructions. *You've each been given an excerpt of writing. Those of you with narrative – turn the passage into a dialogue and action scene. Those with a scene, summarise it into narrative prose.*

TASKSLIP: Narrative

What a glorious spring morning! Red Riding Hood began to pick some flowers along the way to bring to grandmamma. Just as she realised it made an awfully little bouquet, a whiskery, long-jawed gentleman noticed her disappointment and offered advice. Red Riding Hood knew her mother's rules about stranger-danger, but he was polite and proper. He directed her to a clearing where he promised she'd find lots of flowers. Red Riding Hood thanked him and hurried off, certain Mother would be pleased with her thoughtfulness.

TASKSLIP: Scene

Birdsong wove through the sunshine, but Red Riding Hood frowned and sighed. Really, this tiny bunch of snowdrops would hardly do.

'Looking for something more abundant?' a rumbling voice asked.

'Yes! To make my grandmamma feel better.' She gazed up at the whiskery gentleman. What a long face he had.

'Just behind that copse is a clearing full of daffodils.'

'Thank you, sir, but my mother said –'

'She sent you to cheer up your granny, didn't she?'

Red Riding Hood looked again at her scrappy bunch of flowers. 'It's not far, you say?'

He shook his head.

'Mother would allow it just this once,' she decided, and skipped up the trail.

Reading out. The solutions will be many and the familiar tale is good for laughter. Students are always curious to hear the original 'official' narrative and scene of the taskslip they didn't get to see. Some dialogue points will arise (particularly attribution, actions as attribution), as of course will the difference in emotional effect of the two versions. Some students will favour narrative over scene, some will find one or the other difficult to write... In their own work, I've found that most early writers err on the side of narrative. But a few err too far into scene, so it's like reading a film script. The ideal is a balance – tell students to look at the fiction they enjoy reading! In general:

- *Narration for the sake of the story, to move it along, explain, describe, create transition.*
- *Dialogue for the sake of the characters, to display personality, to put the reader right into the story's 'real time' happenings.*

60 EXERCISE: Storyboarding a Scene

Now to get students originating their own scenes. This method is from Robert J Ray's valuable how-to, The Weekend Novelist; it's had a UK update recently and he's also author of seven crime novels. I find it as useful as **Character Profile** for bridging the gap between the empty page and creating real fiction. **Tutor, prepare** the storyboard worksheet as below allowing writing space under each prompt and dropping the italics – they're your talking points as you explain the task.

Storyboard a Scene

To explore a possible scene, slip into it by pre-writing, making notes on each area:

Stage Setup *In movies this is all part of the picture, but writers have to do it in words. Characters can't exist in a vacuum; work through this list and things begin to get real.*

    time/place: *morning, at the breakfast table? midnight, in the ballroom?*

    temperature/season: *spring, a chill drizzle? winter, sparkling snow?*

    lighting/sounds/smells/senses: *sun pouring in, bacon sizzling, toast burnt? chandeliers, candles, waltz, gardenias?*

    props: *cutlery, coffee mugs, cigarette, newspaper? white gloves, fan? What items will characters be touching, seeing, using as they act, talk, interact?*

    symbols/images: *the jam pot Jimmy made when he was five? wilting house plant on the window sill? the glass slipper? the big clock? These may be props, but they are also loaded with meaning – could be the past, or a theme or evidence of a character trait. In early stages you might not know these... just aim for props; as the story grows symbols will emerge.*

Characters/relationships: *Cinderella and Prince... newly enchanted with each other? Frank and Stella, married for one year? Maeve and Jimmy, mother (40) and son (18)? Of course in an on-going story you'll soon know all the characters, so you won't need to storyboard this slot.*

Dialogue: *Don't write the dialogue, just indicate what you will write.*

    subjects: *what they will do/did on the weekend? how lovely the music is?*

    subtext: *What they're really saying under the surface. I'm bored with you? I think I'm pregnant? I'm in love with you?*

Action:

    large: *dancing? leaving the room? dropping a plate? Involves full body and motion.*

    supporting: *smoking? toying with toast crusts? stirring coffee? smoothing own hair? picking up pen? Small actions, often involves props.*

Point of View: *As with character, you'll decide this at the start of your work: through whose eyes will we live this scene?*

Climax: *A scene has to build to a point, then come to a close. If there's no climax to a scene, then nothing's really happening – the story isn't moving along. 'Let's dance all night,' murmured the prince. 'It's midnight, good-bye!' she gasped.*

Ending image, exit line or action (mood): *The wrap-up or aftermath of the climax, often leaves a problem or new development. The 12th chime of midnight, the slipper on the palace stairs; the dirty dishes in the sink, a bud on the pruned plant.*

Tutor, use the storyboard worksheet as an exercise in one or both of the following ways:

Storyboard Plunge variation. Give out worksheet and explain the points. Then tell students to get started with an idea of their own, probably from one of their previous exercises (characters, monologues, dialogues, point of view). Or a character from their own work in progress. Stop and discuss when the worksheet is completed. I find this is enough to experience use of storyboard, but you could have them write the scene in class if there's time, or tell them to carry on at home.

Storyboard Demo variation. Demonstrate on the board with the whole class using a scene they all know, or imagining a scene together. The Cinderella at midnight scene might do, or those two people chatting by the coffee machine mentioned above (or any other scene you've referred to in class). Then turn them loose on the worksheet as in **Storyboard Plunge** above.

61 EXERCISE: The Shape of a Scene

As covered in the **What's a Scene?** mini-lecture, dramatic tension defines a scene: a beginning, a middle that builds to a climax, and then an aftermath and ending. A simple diagram on the board or on a handout demonstrates this. (See **Shape of the Whole Story,** further on, for diagram.)

Hand out the text of a polished, published scene. That scene from The Lilac Bus (see **Dialogue Technicalities,** earlier) is a good example. Ask students to read through and then guide the class in deciding

- *where the beginning becomes middle*
- *what they feel is the climax of tension between the characters*
- *who 'wins'*
- *where does the resolution begin*

You can chart these points on a diagram of rising tension as the group arrives at answers (people may disagree – all good fuel for discussion). Refer to storyboard elements if you've used the **Storyboard** exercise already.

> **TIP: Soften the writing-by-numbers approach**
>
> Mini-lectures, diagrams, structured worksheets and analysis of text can scare off that tender writing urge. Indeed anything in class may do that. I always warn students:
> *These approaches may not work for all, and if this one doesn't appeal to you, fine! Chuck it out, forget it, and, it's true, you cannot write by numbers. Respect your instinct. These are all crutches, tools, to use or not use. It may be best to completely forget about this lesson, let it sink down into your subconscious, where it may serve you well in due course. When you finish a piece, when you are revising it, when you feel instinctively that something is not quite right about a scene, dialogue, character or whatever, THAT's the time to remember these tools, to help you fix your work.*

62 EXERCISE: Groupwork Scene Writing

Scene planning and writing is fun, and in film and tv is often a collaborative effort. Combine storyboarding with the need for dramatic tension in this small group exercise – it makes a very lively session. Pull tables around so you'll have 3 - 4 people in each group, and provide taskslips with a scenario, plus a **Storyboard** worksheet.

TASKSLIP: Scenario (This example is inspired by a children's TV show)

Frankie and Tom prepare to send their pet tortoises on a secret investigation. The tortoises will go under the fence to detect whether the neighbour's poppies are the evil kind they saw on the TV news. Everything's ready, until Frankie discovers that Tom has forgotten the string they need to retrieve the tortoises. They plan to try again the next day and Tom swears not to let Frankie down.

Instructions. Together, each group bounces around ideas to fill in the storyboard, then sketches in dialogue and shape, deciding on the build to the climax. They do not write the scene, just jot notes. Allow about 20 minutes, reminding students to plan the shape (they tend to get carried away with props!); then each group presents to all the others.

What's the point? By working through a scene, even without writing it out, students see just how many possibilities there are, and how dialogue and actions need characters with specific personalities. Use discussion of the results to illustrate good examples, or missed opportunities, for characterisation, actions, setting, props, dialogue and, of course, dramatic tension.

63 EXERCISE: Groupwork Scene Writing (variation)

As above (or invent your own scenario), however, in this variation give each group slightly different character facts. So, using the above example:

- Frankie and Tom are kids, friends aged 11
- Frankie and Tom are brothers, aged 10 and 12
- Frankie and Tom are adults, aged 30-plus
- Frankie is a girl, a tomboy; she and Tom are aged 10

What's the point? The relationships and ages of characters will change the dialogue and some of the action, revealing Frankie and Tom's relationship. The presentation by each group to the whole class is even more fun if the others have to guess the ages and relationships.

MINI-LECTURE 7: The Shape of the Whole Story

With scene-making in mind, it's time to pull back a bit and consider how scenes fit into the full length of a story. The most reliable, effective way to tell a story – be it novel, play, film, narrative poem or short story – is the classic three-act dramatic incline. Each scene alone uses the same structure, simplified as: beginning, middle, end. Over the whole of a work this translates as acts – often invisible to readers, but most definitely felt by them: an arrangement of peak moments. In the Weekend Novelist, Robert J Ray (who is also the author of seven crime novels) calls these major stepping stones key scenes.

The Shape of the Whole Story

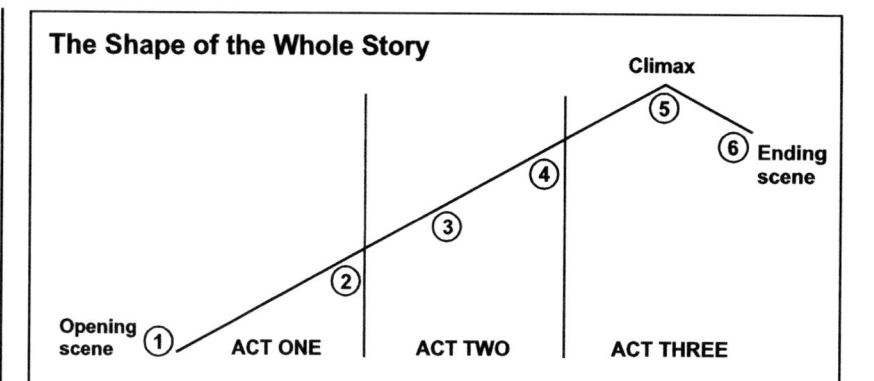

```
                                    Climax
                                      ⑤
                                    /   \
                                   /     ⑥  Ending
                                  ④       \ scene
                                 /
                               ③
                              /
                            ②
                           /
  Opening   /
  scene   ①     ACT ONE  |  ACT TWO  |  ACT THREE
```

Act One – set up

The opening, a scene (Key Scene 1) shows a character with problems that need solutions; intervening scenes introduce other characters, add complications. Finally, at the close of Act One, a scene (Key Scene 2) sets the protagonist new and worse complications. From this point, things will change.

Act Two – middle

Developments, many ups and downs, perhaps some new characters, lead to a scene of a change, a turning point (Key Scene 3). This often comes at about the midpoint of the story; it may be a breakthrough, a revelation, or even a reversal or defeat for the protagonist.

In the second half of Act Two, the hero/heroine deals with the crisis or change of the midpoint, eventually meeting the challenge and reaching a scene of turning point (Key Scene 4).

Act Three – resolution

It has all led to this, a quickened pace now as the hero/ine takes the plunge, the big confrontation (Key Scene 5), the climax of the protagonist's journey or quest. You have catharsis – the release of tension for the hero and the reader – and then the denoument, or wrap up of details. An ending scene (Key Scene 6) gives the reader the final mood, the aftermath of dealing with the problem.

A novel is more than just Key Scenes, of course. Other scenes, and narrative summary, build up to and away from Key Scenes, setting them up, establishing characters, giving backstory, describing, explaining.

Tutor, tips on mini-lecture:

- Diagram the three-act incline on the board as you talk, and give the mini-lecture as a **handout** afterwards.

- It's helpful if the whole class knows a good example in common which you can refer to in your talk – I often use the first Star Wars film, or a short story or novel we've all read (see *Running the Course* section).

- See **Soften the writing-by-numbers approach** a couple of pages back – you don't want to terrify budding storytellers with too much theory. Counterbalance with sheer creativity by scheduling a quick, lively wordplay exercise in the session.

- Having presented the idea of structure you can't just tell students to go write a story; they need new juice, story stimulus, something from **Postcards & Pictures,** perhaps, or **Peer Imperative,** or the story-making exercises **Rainbow Tales, Plunge into Action, Agony Letter.** There's also that character and his family, friends and rivals, from the **Character Profile,** and further ahead, **Deeper into Character** exercises. And/or use one of the following two staged exercises.

64 EXERCISE: Plotting by Key Scenes

This exercise works directly from the **Shape of the Story** mini-lecture. A criss-cross procedure suggested by crime writer Robert J Ray's book The Weekend Novelist, I've found that just telling students is not effective, yet they respond with creative success to dictation in stages – must be the element of surprise that helps. Allow time for writing after each stage.

Preamble to students: *You have a story in mind, something that you have barely begun working on, or an idea you'd like to work on. Visualise, feel your way into these scenes as I prompt you. Don't worry about specific details, just jot down setting, characters, dialogue notes and actions.*

Stage 1. *The opening. What scene would show the protagonist and his/her problem(s)?* (Key Scene 1)

Stage 2. *The final mood. What scene would show happiness, sadness, bitterness... the aftermath of the story?* (Key Scene 6)

Stage 3. *The midpoint. What could be a major discovery or reversal for the protagonist? Give it a setting, actions, characters, dialogue.* (Key Scene 3)

Stage 4. *Going back to the end of Act 1, after getting to know the main characters and problems, what scene, what action or event could set your character going into new and worse complications?* (Key Scene 2)

Stage 5. *Jump ahead: your hero/ine has been meeting the challenge of the midpoint. Think of a scene that shows him/her reaching a turning point, closure or decision.* (Key Scene 4, end of Act Two)

Stage 6. *The climax. The big confrontation, the scene that shows him or her dealing with the problem at the start and the other complications.* (Key Scene 5)

Tutor, no reading out after this exercise, just check for responses – there's usually an 'aha!' feeling in the class, a sense of, 'hey, this story could work!' By prompting students to start with a story they have vaguely in mind you are using the energy of their own idea, freeing stalled creativity. Thinking in jumbled, isolated key scenes helps them to dramatize a story idea, finding the stepping stones without worrying about the joining-up bits. Urge students to go ahead and write the story at home. (IF you have time, you could have students begin to write their opening scene in class, but it's not essential to the exercise.)

For more analysis of plotting, scene and structure, see discussion guidelines in **Reading for Writers** in *Running the Course* section.

65 EXERCISE: Opening with the Ending

This is an experience in structure, scene and a few other craft points as well. You can use it instead of the exercise above, but don't use both in succession as they are too similar in method. This is also good when talking about openings, or simply as a story stimulus. I adapted it from Fiction Writer's Workshop by Josip Novakovich. He meant it for the novel, but it works as well for short story. The aim is to get the feel of grasping a whole, beginning to end. Allow a good 30 - 40 minutes for this so that students can write at some length. Dictate it in stages allowing time to write after each step.

Stage 1. *Write a one page scene set at a wedding or a funeral.*

Stage 2. *Write a one page scene that jumps back in time to 'how it all began', a scene involving a key person in the first scene.*

Stage 3. *Outline, quickly and broadly, the stages of the relationships and events that could develop following the scene you've just written, involving the key people: stepping stones of ups, downs, obstacles, struggles, triumphs, failure.*

Stage 4. *Write the story's very last paragraph. Chronologically it is the stage just before, or inevitably leading to, the wedding or funeral that opens the story. It need not be a full scene: a telling thought, image or sense can work well.*

Tutor, briefly air students' reactions to the exercise, then **read out.** The story comes full circle because opening with the last events makes both a starting point and a goal for the narrative. This is helpful to the writer – a light at the end of the tunnel! – as well as a tried-and-true storytelling device for readers. Tell students: *if this turns into a story you want to write, or if you use this device for a different story idea, once you draft it fully you can try cutting out that first wedding/funeral scene, you may not need it.*

MINI-LECTURE 8: The Character's Journey

This concept-and-demonstration, like the others in the **Scene and Plot** series, gives writers an over-arching grasp of story structure, this time fully based on character. Here is a handout, but talk it through before distributing. Then follow with the lively small group exercise.

The Character's Journey

The heart of good plot and story is a character (or several) who can sustain a journey through a whole work. Readers engage with a character who will develop and be changed. Noah Lukeman, in The Plot Thickens, says there are two kinds of journey for your main character: profound and surface. Each kind has several different possibilities. Successful stories set the character simultaneously on surface and profound journeys.

The Profound Journey of inner change is usually not overtly action-dramatic, but is most deeply satisfying to the reader. Lukeman describes themes:

Profound Journey # 1: Realisation About Others. Waking up and seeing people for who they really are, or a situation for what it is.

Profound Journey # 2: Self-realisation. Recognising that something inside of him/her led him/her into a negative or untruthful situation, protagonist gains internal identity and takes responsibility for this.

Profound Journey # 3: Taking Action Based on Realisation. Resolution: a character sees the truth, realises she/he has some power and responsibility, and takes action to change self and/or situation. This last journey goes through all three stages and is the most satisfying, but any of the above can be the journey and lead to the ending of a successful story. Or the three stages can provide a structure over the length of a story.

The Surface Journey is visible and active, concerned with the outer world, as described by Lukeman. 'Rags to riches' and 'boy meets girl' are two of the most common journeys. Several surface journeys can be combined in the same story; journeys can be successes or reversals. However, if a character's life changes externally, but leads to no inner, profound, realisations about self and others, then it's not a satisfying story – or it's a tragedy. The best stories see the character through both journeys, the surface journey forcing the profound change.

Surface Journey # 1: Romance (or separation)

Surface Journey # 2: Material Gain (or loss)

Surface Journey # 3: Friendships (or enemies)

Surface Journey # 4: Physical (overcoming odds, or losing advantage)

Surface Journey # 5: Knowledge (from ignorance to knowledge, or the perils of knowledge)

Surface Journey # 6: Stature (or loss of, in business, society…)

Surface Journey # 7: Family (getting it, keeping it, losing it)

In setting out to write, story works best if character has a specific goal for his perceived surface journey… BUT character can take detours, waver, change his mind, turn back. Eg, sets out for India, but gets out in Istanbul. These switches can involve external, surface elements and/or internal realisations.

66 EXERCISE: The Character's Journey

Now bring the mini-lecture to life by putting students into small groups of 3 or 4, and giving out worksheets (half-page is enough). Give a copy to each student in the group, but each group has its own different story start.

Worksheet 1:

Character's Journey – a married woman
Story start/situation: a married woman locates an ex-boyfriend via email
Goal:
Obstacles to achieving goal; conflicts, struggles, ups&downs:
The final struggle/conflict:
Resolution (goal achieved? not achieved?):
Possible profound journey(s):

Instructions. *Each group brainstorms the elements of the story – characters, motives, locations etc. Sketch in the whole character journey. The goal and obstacles, of course, is the surface journey. What will be the character's profound journey, what learned about others, self? Any action taken as a result? Discuss and devise for 15 minutes, then each group will relate their story to the whole class.*

Three further Character's Journey situations. Prepare as the worksheet above. If you have more than four groups it is fine to give the same situation to two groups – creativity ensures that the stories developed will be different.

Worksheet 2. Story start/situation: paralysed man offered a break-through operation allowing him to walk

Worksheet 3. Story start/situation: a runaway teen returns after two years and finds another family living in the family home

Worksheet 4. Story start/situation: a redundant worker decides prospects will be better in another part of the country

Tutor. This is a lively exercise without individual writing that may take 20 minutes in group work, then 20 minutes in whole group (you could have coffee break in between). If a group does not get all the way through their story that's fine, it's all to illustrate the possibilities of story, and the need for inner as well as outer change in character. During the tellings-out interject praise, alternatives and possible improvements or missed opportunities as a way of elaborating on the mini-lecture.

VI. STORYTELLING DEVICES

As well as the big strokes of story-making – character, scene, plot – close-up crafting can be practised and improved. The following craft exercises can stand alone, mixed in with other activities in a session, or you can run them in series – three weeks of openings exercises, for instance, or two sessions of characterisation. Choose as suits your interests or issues which arise in class.

67 EXERCISE: Matching Openings

To stimulate discussion about what makes a good opening, find a half-dozen or so novels or short story openings that you like (select text of not more than six lines) and copytype them to make paired taskslip handouts. (See **Pairing Devices** in *Stimulus* section for more on the exercise method.) Students find their matching quote, and the pair must decide what elements work (or don't) in this opening. After 5 minutes or so call the class into one large group and list on the board as many opening devices as possible from the examples. Reveal author and title as a reward for each contribution.

68 EXERCISE: Openings – Write On!

Also using copytyped examples of openings (so it might follow on the **Matching Openings** exercise... or not), distribute taskslips of opening texts and set the exercise: *Continue the story.* Allow time for a page of writing. After students **read out** the exercise reveal original authors and how their text continued.

69 EXERCISE: Modelling Openings

One way to write better openings is to walk in the shoes of a master. Again, copytype openings as handouts. Hand out the taskslips and instruct students: *Study the opening, then follow the author's pattern by modelling after him or her. Change words, but not the sentence construction, in order to create a different story with the same opening style.*

Students usually ask anxiously about how to proceed; answer as seems best, but mainly just urge them forward. Here's my modelled version of the opening of Dashiel Hammet's The Thin Man to illustrate the process (but don't do this in full for students, the lesson is in the discovery of doing):

> I was slouching over the counter in a Starbucks on the Portobello Road, waiting for Ruby to bargain over antique nightgowns, when a dude walked away from the queue where he'd been ordering take-aways with two other blokes and came over to me. He was tall and spike-haired, and whether you looked at his nose or at his arms in tattoo'd splendour, the result was unsettling. 'Aren't you King Jake?' he demanded.

Reading out: Plenty of opportunity for discussion of tone, hooks, character and setting as the substituted modelling brings about changes. Encourage students who are intrigued with their new opening to turn it into a full story; emphasise to all that this is a tool they can use at any time, and that the borrowed opening can be edited out, if they wish, once the story is fully drafted.

70 EXERCISE: Imperative Opening

Of course an opening is only relevant to the story that follows, and every piece your students have written so far has an opening. Still, once you have aired a variety of opening modes via one or two of the exercises above, you can have students practice openings. I am loathe to have students tinker with their own work-in-progress for the sake of class exercises – if a writer has embarked on something genuinely his or her own, the work is not then to be toyed with. Therefore, draw upon some of the previous exercises, part-stories created in class from, say, **Character's Journey, Opening with an Ending,** the pet tortoise **Scenario, Rainbow Tale, Agony Letter, Character Profile,** or even **Red Riding Hood.** Choose one that will be fairly fresh in students' minds, or remind them of several recent exercises so they can choose their own. Prepare the following handout, which also serves as a taskslip:

> **Some Ways to Open a Story**
> - Dialogue
> - Setting description – landscape, weather or geography
> - Setting description – interior
> - Monologue, first person
> - Character description, third person
> - Characters in action

Instructions. Get students to have an exercise part-story in mind, then hand out the taskslip. Go round and tick one item on each person's list – a different item for each student. (Repeat the cycle for however many students you have.)

With your story in mind, write an opening in the mode I've ticked, about a half page long. Remember to bubble first, to help you expand and gather your thoughts. (See **Bubble** in *Stimulus* section.)

After **reading out** and discussing, if you wish to extend the exercise you can do another round of ticks, forcing students to stretch themselves into devising a different manner of opening with the same story in mind. Or you can let them choose their own option from the list. When they moan, say: *Yes, you must stick with the same story, the better to explore the effect!*

What about endings? Because you need a whole story before you can end it, and because I believe in the creative sacredness of a student's own whole piece as stated above, I've yet to devise a useful exercise. The main ways to develop better ending-craft is via whole-story work in the **Scene and Plot** exercises, and via **Reading for Writers** (discussion of published work) and **Workshopping** students' own work – see *Running the Course* for these methods.

71 EXERCISE: Flashback

If good stories are based on character, and characters' actions are based on motive… we are into the backstory of a story, some event or circumstance in the past affecting characters in the now of the story. Flashback is familiar through TV, film and fiction. Several craft issues here: how to find the past event, how to write it, how to weave it into the story. This exercise addresses the first two.

Stage 1. *Take a small piece of paper, write on it a name for a character – first name alone is okay, or full name if you want. Fold it over to hide it, pass to your neighbour.*

Stage 2. *Without looking at the name, write an age on the paper, anywhere between 8 and 80. Now crumple up the paper and put them in the kitty...* (You go round with a bag, box or basket) *...and now draw one out.*

Stage 3. *Now open up your character paper. Do a chronology of this person's life – the NOW of the story is our own present time, today's date and year. Work out what year the person was born, what year he or she started school, when education finished.*

Stage 4. Tutor now offers one or other of the following writing exercises, or a choice of either or... or one, followed by the other.

- *Your character's first love, first romance or first sex: what age was he/she, what year did this happen? Describe the episode and the other person involved.*

- *Someone in your character's life died. What age was your character, what year was it? Who died? Describe your character's reaction to this, and his/her relationship with the dead person.*

Read out. Use the feedback to discuss deepening of character and possibilities for story structure and handling of entering and leaving flashback.

Flashback Transition Tips

– Avoid the had-hads: once you get into the past, use the simple past tense

– Signal return to present story by saying Now or repeating an action, dialogue, or object that occurred just before the flashback

– Gap or centred asterisk on the page is a classic transition device

– Contrasting weather or items can help clarify ('this box was porcelain, that one was cracked leatherette but it held...')

Flashback follow-on. Use **Ritual & Reverie,** further on in **Richer Writing** exercises, for practice in writing flashback and weaving it into a story.

VII. DEEPER INTO CHARACTER

72 EXERCISE: Deeper into Character – The Scar

Following **Character Profile** (see earlier in *Craft* section) or any other character or story work, or springboarding from **Flashback,** you can go deeper into a character's past by discovering that the character has a scar. Give students a moment to get in mind one of their own created characters or an exercise character, then instruct them, allowing time to write after each question:

Your character has a scar somewhere on his or her body. Is it visible, or hidden? Where is it? Is it large or small? How long ago was the injury? What happened? Describe the incident, including other people who were or might have been present. How does your character feel about the scar now? Start her or him thinking about it.

Read out – it's amazing how many directions a scar can take you. This can be yet another way into flashback for insights into character, or it may well be the central point of a story. If you prefer, use the following exercise instead.

73 EXERCISE: Deeper into Character – Dream

Drop in this spontaneous exercise any time during a course to lighten up and get people writing free. Students need to have a character in mind, and you need a set of your **Postcards** (see *Stimulus* section), probably surreal ones, or possibly situation or mythical pictures – nothing too realistic, because you want to trigger the illogical dream world. And for the surprise second stage, you'll need different postcards or your **Serendipity Bag.** If you want, preamble this in the session, or in the previous session, with the **Vivid Verbs** exercise (see *Richer Writing)* to loosen creativity.

Stage 1. Spread out the picture-cards and allow students to choose one each.

Instructions. *You have a character in mind, either one in your own work that you are developing, or one from one of our exercises. This character has a dream, based on the card you've just chosen. Start writing the dream, remembering that it can shift and change and not make sense, as dreams do.*

Stage 2. After they have been writing for a little while, go round and put a Serendipity Bag item or a new postcard at each person's place. Say, *This is a shift in the dream, incorporate it into the character's dream.*

Read out: Ideally, colourful and improbable images and events will emerge. Tell students that it is a tool – the dream may or may not become part of a story. Either way, it is a route to exploring and revealing character.

MINI-LECTURE 9: Characterization

As well as glimpsing the inner workings of characters, good writing brings characters alive by SHOWING them to the reader, not just telling in abstract summary terms, such as 'Henry was an optimist' or 'Sarah hated being short'. Good characterisation uses all sorts of attributes to let readers know the nature of the character without flat 'case history' type descriptions. **Tutor,** give some examples from a few authors to illustrate this lecture and handout. An exercise follows.

5 FORMS OF CHARACTERISATION

Bring characters alive by <u>showing</u> them to the reader.

1. Physical description: height, hair, eye colour, skin, girth, posture, teeth, earlobes... other
2. Speaking (dialogue): what is said, how it is said, quality of voice, accent, speech patterns...
3. Actions: small, large, mannerisms...
4. Association of items

    Clothes and possessions that give clues (ever-present umbrella, dangly earrings…)

    Also, the state of these items (new/old, clean/dirty, expensive/cheap...)
5. Other characters talk or think about a character

74 EXERCISE: Characterization Challenge

To follow the mini-lecture above prepare a set of word cards, each with a single character trait. Explain before you distribute one to each student: *We want to bring characters alive by showing them to the reader. The following descriptions are excellent character traits, BUT, how would the reader know without being told in a summary word by you that a person is like this?*

Without using the word or phrase on the card, write a half page <u>showing</u> a character with this trait – include dialogue, make it a scene. Afterwards we'll read out and see if the class can determine the original trait.

Words for the cards: vain; shy; laid back; needs to be centre of attention; brave; a poseur; principled; cynical about life; scatter-brained; ambitious... (go on and add as many as you need).

Reading out usually includes lots of laughter as a troupe of exaggerated characters peoples the room, and each writer gets the fun of playing quiz master to his/her character sketch.

VIII. RICHER WRITING EXERCISES

Some close-up craftwork should dwell on the sheer joy of words, with exercises to enrich the texture of writing. Ideally students' grammar and punctuation are satisfactory – if not, as tutor, comment gently in the margins of work handed in, and if necessary suggest remedial work (perhaps your institution offers such classes). I've decided it's not my role to teach grammar, and besides, though I know what's right, I don't always know how to explain why – teaching grammar requires specific training. But if commas stray or other errors occur, I mostly just grit my teeth: creativity's the thing. The following exercises, which cross several crafting areas, mainly aim to nudge students out of routine ruts of writing.

75 EXERCISE: Descriptive Powers

This is a fast, fun word substitution exercise adapted from a language teaching book, Five-Minute Activities. A pass-around participation, prepare taskslips of vertically halved A4 sheets: a sentence at the top, and half the alphabet beneath.

TASKSLIP: Descriptive Powers
  My neighbour's cat is an <u>awful</u> cat.
  a
  b
  c
  etc to **m**

The word to be substituted is underlined. Another sheet is headed with the same sentence with the letters n – z beneath. This makes two long vertical strips to hand out, and here are some more sentences (make up as many as you need; some duplication is fine).

- Her voice was as <u>soft</u> as her face.
- The painting <u>astonished</u> the critics.
- You are <u>taller</u> than I am.
- The door of the house is <u>shabby.</u>

Instructions. *Replace the underlined word with another which starts with the alphabet letter next on the list. Do just one, then pass it on to the next person, as a very fast round. If you get the same sentence that's okay, because you'll be on another letter. If you get totally stuck choose any other blank letter on the list. Poetic license is encouraged*!

As tutor, keep the papers moving around quickly, don't let anyone dither long – it's just an exercise! Everyone ends with a completed sheet.

Read out. Borrow a sheet and read out, dramatizing with tone of voice as suits the words. Have everyone read out – you'll all marvel at the richness and power a single word can impart.

76 EXERCISE: Ritual & Reverie

Here's a multi-layered, longish exercise that works in senses, tenses, character and flashback – and it's fun, too! The seed of the idea is from Robert J Ray's The Weekend Novelist. Don't reveal the whole of it in advance.

Stage 1 (2 - 3 minutes). *Ritual is a process repeated over and over, sometimes with sacred significance. However, ritual is also part of daily* life, not sacred usually, but repetitive, semi-absorbing, an activity that distracts you and allows you to think. Some examples: cooking, driving, fishing, sewing, bathing, washing up, applying makeup, shaving, exercising, weeding, walking the dog...

List three of your own, or a character's, rituals.

Stage 2 (5 minutes). *Choose one, and bubble on it, remembering the **8 senses** (see **Stimulus** section), jotting all you can think of that happens during this routine action. (Pause as they get started.) As you do this, one of these actions or senses will remind you of something – go on and bubble a little on this.*

Stage 3 (3-4 minutes). *Stop now, and look over the ritual action. Write two sentences in present tense, which start to take you (or the character) through the routine.*

Stage 4 (3-4 minutes). *Now write a few sentences about the thing that you (or the character) were reminded of – write this in past tense.*

Stage 5 (5-10 minutes). *Stop, and go back to two more sentences in the present tense experience of the routine. Continue, switching back and forth between ritual and recollection, present tense and past tense.*

Read out and discuss. What's the point? Besides the tenses exercise, ritual and reverie can deepen scenes and character, connect events, link narrative or backstory. The ritual can soothe and affirm the memories... or it might fail, creating or showing disturbance. These passages can also provide images and symbols.

Follow-up Ritual & Reverie. If the class is interested, you can try putting the ritual in past tense and the memory in present tense, to see the difference in effect. Ritual and reflection can all be in the same tense, too.

MINI-LECTURE 10: Setting

Setting is, of course, vital to any flight of writing when you want to put the reader right into the experience. It can also be almost another character in a story, a force and presence to reckon with. But pure descriptive passages can clog a piece – the downside of writing too richly.

- *One of the best ways to avoid slowing the pace is to show the setting through the character's eyes and responses instead of the author's straightforward 'telling'.*
- *Subtext is a related dual-duty device – use setting but colour it with the tone or attitude of the character. This advances the story as it paints the scene.*

Tutor: if you want to spend more time on setting, you can have students study published texts using the **Matching Openings** method a few pages back, and/or use some writing exercises from **8 Senses Travel** or **Pictures**, or **Life-Listing** places, found in *Stimulus* section. I began to find pure setting exercises falling flat, except for the one below, and think it may be best to keep setting as part of story.

77 EXERCISE: Setting & Subtext

After the setting mini-lecture in which you have defined subtext (the term is also used in **Storyboarding**, applied to dialogue), introduce this two-stage exercise – don't reveal that there is a second stage.

Stage 1 (5-10 minutes). *Describe a lake as seen by a man who has just learned of his wife's infidelity. Do not mention the wife, love, jealousy, her lover, sex, marriage or infidelity.*

Read out. Look for the negative, sad or angry tone expressed through what the character sees, feels and does. Then spring the next step on your students.

Stage 2 (5-10 minutes). *Describe the same lake, same weather, same time of day as seen by a man who has just proposed marriage to and been accepted by the woman he loves. Do not mention the woman, love, sex or marriage.*

Read out and appreciate the difference.

Alternative situation: (1) Describe a lake (or river) as seen by a woman who has just learned that she is pregnant and she is happy about it. Do not mention the pregnancy or the father of the baby. (2) Describe a lake (or river) as seen by a woman unhappy to have learned that she is pregnant. Do not mention the pregnancy or the father of the baby.

78 EXERCISE: Transcribing Tenses

The issues of tenses usually comes up when discussing **Point of View**, and it is part of the flashback aspect of **Ritual & Reverie**, but you can delve into it as a separate topic. Get students to play with the effects of tense in one of the following exercises.

Transcribing Tenses – published text. Copytype 2-4 short passages of published fiction in past and present tenses and photocopy as taskslips. Students transcribe them: present to past, past to present.

You can do this in two stages, giving out all past tense samples to start, then discussing the effect of past-into-present, then setting students to work on the present-to-past samples. Or you can do them all at once, alternating the distribution round the room.

Transcribing Tenses – own text variation. Instead of given texts, you can use a *Stimulus* exercise to generate a half page of writing. Do this before discussing tenses so that students instinctively write in past tense – perhaps one of the **Life-Listing** exercises, or something with an **I remember** start. Then introduce the idea of present tense and instruct them to rewrite, changing the verbs.

Some students will ask: As students begin to write, you'll find they remark with surprise how the tense change sometimes forces other changes in the writing; encourage them to make whatever adjustments necessary.

Reading out. Invite comments on how tone is affected. Lead students to form judgements on the pros and cons of each tense. Present tense writing can open discussion on contemporary cutting-edge fiction.

79 EXERCISE: Adjectives/Adverbs – Style & Genre

Purple prose – or not. Prepare this re-writing exercise as a full-page double-spaced worksheet to allow room for editing, then turn students loose as editors.

Adjectives/Adverbs Rewrite

Delete as many adjectives/adverbs as possible in the passage below:

Silvery moonlight pierced the thick green canopy formed by the branching limbs of the ancient oak trees and gently dappled the century-old marble monument that stood, forlorn and abandoned in the remotest corner of the silent graveyard.

Insert some adjectives/adverbs in the passage below:

Pushing her way among the overhanging weeds, many of which were covered with blossoms, Mary found herself a seat on a rock that had been rolled against the trunk of an old apple tree. The weeds half concealed her and from the road only her head was visible. A hedge separated the orchard from the fields on the hillside. Mary intended to sit by the tree until darkness came creeping over the land and to try to think out some plan regarding her future.

Decide which adjectives/adverbs are worth keeping in the passage below and remove the rest:

The summer idle water mirrored the towering cliff in a tea-brown pool, and in a small low cave at the crumbling base of the cliff, the soft grey birds were huddled tightly together.

Read out. This provokes lively debate – and hoots of laughter – at the over-the-top or minimalist results. How much description is needed? What is essential, what not? There's no right answer, it's a question of effect. Here you can raise the issue of style and genre. **What's the point?** Tell students this is to raise their awareness of their own use of adjectives and adverbs, particularly when re-writing. If desired, you can continue with a series of genre style studies, reading extracts or whole works in, say, crime, science fiction, high literary fiction, contemporary mainstream fiction etc.

80 EXERCISE: Style & Voice

To develop your own voice – that is, your writing expressed in your own unique style – you have to write a lot. Lots and lots, trying to say what you want to say in the personally best way you can. So can you teach it? Well, you can at least illustrate voice and, as with **Modelling Openings,** you can let your students walk in the shoes of a master to develop a feel for options, to stretch their normal styles.

Preparation. Copytype or photocopy short passages from two distinctively different authors you like. The texts should be ten lines or so, even a half page, so that something of the story moves along. The exercise is in two stages, but don't reveal this.

Instructions. Hand out the excerpts to students; read and discuss the differences in the voices (see if they can guess the authors, if you've chosen famous ones). Then the writing exercise:

Stage 1. *Choose one of the passages, and following word by word, sentence by sentence as exactly as you can, make the passage be about this classroom, this building. You can change the gender of characters if you want, but keep sentence construction, verb tense, positions of adjectives and adverbs exactly as the model.*

Read out. People find this an enjoyable challenge, and are surprised by how it feels to write differently.

Stage 2. Now for something really devious. *Okay, you probably chose the style you personally prefer, or maybe you chose your antithesis because you're a rebel. Now the challenge is to model after the other! See how it feels to stretch yourself the other way.*

You'll get good humoured grumbles, and more good discussion. If you like, you can offer three or four different texts. **What's the point?** As well as exploring style options, tell students they can do this any time they feel stuck, just to experience a half-page flow of being Nabokov, Trapido or any of their favourite authors.

81 EXERCISE: Vivid Verbs

This wordplay from Natalie Goldberg's Writing Down the Bones is one of my favourite exercises, but it's also a scary one, because of the resistance students experience. You will coach them through, but wait til you're good and comfortable with the class. Instruct the students, and demonstrate as you go along:

1. Take a full sheet of paper. Fold it in half vertically, like this. Open it out, so you now have two columns.

2. On the left, write the numbers 1 – 10, in a column. At the top, write the word <u>nouns.</u> Now, think of ten random items, objects, and write them in. You can look around the room or think of your journey here – any thing, any physical, touchable thing, that you think of.

3. Fine. Now, on the right, list the numerals 1 – 15 in a column. At the top, write the word <u>verbs</u>. Now, think of an occupation, preferably something with some physicality to it, such as a chef, an acrobat, a golfer etc. Now fill in 15 verbs, action words, involved in this occupation. So a chef might include slice, stir, chop, sauté and so forth.

4. Okay, so now you have two columns of words. The task is to make ten sentences using a noun from the left column and one of the verbs from the right. You can complete the sentence as you like, but you must use the noun with one of the action words. You can make things plural or past tense if you want to, but the emphasis is on the verbs. You will probably find it difficult – we are looking for the vivid, the surprising, even the surreal!

Tutor note: students do find this hard to understand, so you can read out a couple of examples – see below, and do your own! Two tips to add as they begin:

- No, you do not have to use all the verbs, there are 5 extra, because this IS hard to do, and they won't all work.
- If you feel yourself struggling, if it seems crazy or impossible, that's natural. You are experiencing the battle of logical, left-brained rational thinking, v free, right-brained creativity – in the interest of fresher, livelier writing.

Examples (acrobat was the occupation I used for the verbs):
- <u>Houses time</u> the next generation.
- <u>Cups practiced</u> at being held in saucers.
- The <u>plane dangles</u> dangerously.
- <u>Engines leap</u> into action.

Reading out. You'll get moans and grumbles, but maintain the reassurance. *Of course not all of the sentences delight, and some don't work, but among them, don't you find one or two that surprise and please you?* (Tutor: if necessary, read out one or two of your new sentences, done just now in the exercise along with the class. Include one you don't like, and say that you don't, and one you do. Encouragement via imperfection!) *Let's hear some of yours.*

What's the point? Promise students that though they may hate these sentences now, if they look again in a month's time they'll be amazed at how good some are. As well as stretching language this exercise demonstrates how very tough the internal critic is (see *Process* section). You might support the lesson by reading a poem or prose that uses strong, unusual wordplay. Of course not every verb needs to be vividly original, but raising awareness helps writers wake up to the power of words.

IX. DIP INTO POETRY

A general beginners' creative writing class might include poetry, drama and creative non-fiction writing, but I've concentrated on what most students expect: story-making. However, at any level and in any discipline, a bit of poetry is useful for a change of pace and for wordplay. You may want to start by distributing copies of a short, good poem you like. If you don't know where to find some, then don't teach poetry! Copytype and distribute, read aloud, and elicit responses. If no responses are forthcoming (among shy beginners), launch into one or both poetry mini-lectures, below, as you estimate students require. They are in the form of talking points; you can use a poem or two to illustrate, and use the whiteboard or handouts to summarise. See also the *Stimulus* exercise **Line from a Poem.**

11 MINI-LECTURE: Elements of a Poem

- Words ordered in lines on a page, rather than in a continuous sequence
- Concentrated, purposeful use of language
- Images –
    - specifics, concrete detail
    - ideas and feelings expressed via the physical world
- Triggers a response

12 MINI-LECTURE: Reading a Poem

ONCE – Do you like it? Not like it? Do you get the gist and meaning, what it's about?

TWICE – LOOK for the shape, for stanzas, an order. Is there any reason why it is arranged this way? A pattern to it? Is punctuation used to a purpose?

THREE TIMES – LOOK & LISTEN for rhyme, line-endings, sounds, language, key words, repetitions of words, placement of words. Read it aloud to hear rhythm. Does any of this specially help the meaning?

NOW – What meaning do you make of it? The opening, the end, the flow and pattern of meaning.

Guided appreciation of any poem, and stimulus into writing a poem, perhaps across a range of themes, can be done once a month, once a term... or only once! Beyond this, there's so much you can say, study and write: the many poetic forms and their advantages, the power of sound and rhythm, the economy and detail of content... but then that's a whole poetry course and a whole book of poetry exercises. So here are just two exercises, one for the 'but how come it's a poem' questioner, and one which might be an end of term creative entertainment.

82 EXERCISE: Free Verse – Why Is It a Poem?

Some students feel mystified by poetry. This analysis, followed by writing exercises, makes a comfortable introduction, with plenty for existing poets to profit by.

Preparation. Choose a short free verse poem you like (maximum about

12 lines), something that seems at first glance to have no rhyme, no particular pattern, and language that feels natural, fairly conversational and 'non-poetic'. Photocopy or copytype it, always crediting the poet and source, of course. Then retype it as prose.

Stage 1. Distribute both versions, read out and discuss the original. Then discuss its effect as straight prose. Which works best to deliver meaning? Point out the power of line-endings, of enjambment, of short v longer lines – together discover what makes this a poem instead of prose.

Stage 2. Do a **Bubble and Riff** exercise (*Stimulus* section), from a word, an object, a sound, a stone, a postcard – whatever strikes your fancy. At the **riff** stage suggest students write phrases instead of prose and then shape them into a free verse poem.

Read out and enjoy... do emphasise that these are raw poems, and students may want to refine them at home over several sessions, allowing time to aid the revising process.

83 EXERCISE: Cinquain

How to introduce form to people who may never be interested in writing poetry? Sonnets require explanations of rhyme schemes, metre, stanzas... too complex for starters. Limericks offer easy rhythm and rhyme, but limit depth of meaning. Here's a simple, little known form which uses no rhyme.

Shower	**Passing Time**
Clean me!	Waiting.
Turn the tap on	Time passes by
the hot steaming water	a relentless journey
trickles down my back to my toes.	a circular continuum.
I'm wet.	Tick tock.

Stage 1. Hand out the two sample cinquains by Katherine Kerr to read and begin to discuss. *Are they poems? Do you like them? What is it that makes them poems?* Lead the discussion on to form, perhaps giving brief definitions of other forms – sonnet, limerick, ballad, haiku – and how form forces the poet into being more precise, the work more effective. Then, in pairs or as a whole group, puzzle out the...

Rules of the Cinquain form

- 5 lines
- Unrhymed
- Instead of syllable beats (word rhythms), a simple syllable count shapes each line:

>line 1 – 2 syllables
>line 2 – 4 syllables
>line 3 – 6 syllables
>line 4 – 8 syllables
>line 5 – 2 syllables

Finally, credit the inventor, Adelaide Crapsey, an American. Discussion will note that the last line has a sort of kick to it.

Stage 2. Then, using a theme or stimulus, set the class writing their own cinquains. A seasonal reference is fun – Valentine's Day, Halloween, spring, summer. You can even distribute 2-syllable taskslips which students must use as their start, like: Sparkling, Winter, Christmas, Present, Trees sway, Shining, New Year. Remind students to **bubble** before going straight to writing. **Read out** and enjoy.

What's the point? For non-poetry-minded students, emphasise that working to find precise words to express idea and emotion in poetry will aid their language in prose. Also, who knows, one of their fiction characters may be moved to write a poem!

X. FIXING A STORY

Writing is re-writing – this is a point you must gently, continually hammer home, but short of the **Transcribing** and **Adjective/Adverb** exercises you can't force students to re-write. The joy is when, as a result of your individual feedback and from workshopping his or her own writing (see *Running the Course)*, a student revises and improves a piece. Drafting, fixing and polishing are part of the *Process* of being a writer – see next section for support on this. Remind students of the **Scene and Plot** exercises when structural help is needed. Here's a specifically revision – or revival – exercise I've found, adapted from

Damon Knight's Creating Short Fiction; it really helps people. No reading out after this, but allow time for students to air their responses to the experience.

84 EXERCISE: Tunnel Vision

When we are stuck with a story it's often because we begin with a tunnel view of it. We think of the beginning and write, a bright disk at the start, a grey tunnel stretching away. We are seeing and feeling it as we do when it will be read. And we tend to bog down or battle on to reach the end. To beat this, you need to look at your story crossways, look at it from the side.

Get a story in mind, one you've left because it's fizzled out, or it's complete but you feel it's weak, something's wrong. Or you can try this with a new, barely developed story idea. Write in response to these steps.

1. Think of one vivid image, a picture of something, a place, item or person at the beginning of the story. Write it, really vivid and detailed.

2. Okay, now, envision and write a vivid image for the end.

3. Now, that soggy middle. Another vivid image. Look around in the story's world, what do you see? Books, carpets, house plants? Who else is in the room, or next door? Who is important to your character? Who do they love or hate? Jot, bubble or list some of these.

4. Look back into the past of your main character. What was an experience that influenced her or him now? What is a secret they never told? Write this in 1-3 sentences.

5. What does the story mean? Does the ending support the meaning? If not, you need a different ending. Dare to list some alternative endings – an opposite, a stronger version, a milder version, a variation, something completely other?

So, now you need to go back and forth along the tunnel of your story to make all of these new parts fit. Thank goodness for word processors – fix, smooth, polish: you are rewriting!

Section 4

PROCESS: Living the writing life

I. Teaching Writing/Growing People

II. Into the Writing World

Section 4

PROCESS: Living the Writing Life

99.9% of new writers will come to your class with the not-so-secret agenda: *I want to be a writer,* meaning *I want to write and be published, famous and rich.* As a working writer you know: writing is hard work, getting published is tough and getting rich unlikely. But you need to break this news gently, maintaining enthusiasm as well as introducing realities.

This section contains practicalities on two very different aspects of being a writer. First, the processes of writing: how to get started, how to keep going. Second, pointers on getting published. Some students aim to go the whole distance into mainstream publishing, many never send work into the wider world. As a nurturing tutor with a successful class (defined as retaining students for the whole run of the course) you want to provide support and keep your writers fulfilling themselves, published or not.

I. TEACHING WRITING/GROWING PEOPLE

As you teach writing you are also growing the artist within, leading the student to discover his or her own voice – that is, the part that wants to create, to speak, to make. As a writer yourself you've experienced the struggle, and as a tutor you will sense and hear the problems: *Why can't I do it more, more often, better? I never have enough time. I don't know where to start. I have too many ideas. I don't have enough ideas. I started but then I got stuck. I always start but never finish. I finish but I hate re-writing. I finish but I never submit. I got criticised/rejected and I'll never write again.* These are not issues of writing craft, they are needs for work on the self, the artist self.

What follows here are tools to help the writer write. You'll use the first two **Toolkits** early in the course, to warm and loosen your writers. Then drop the others in, more or less in order, or as you feel ready; pick and choose, you needn't run them all in one course. Read them, try them yourself and balance each session with upbeat exercises as these are very lecturey, aimed at stirring insight. Some exercises venture slightly into psychological territory; see **Sensitive Flowers** in *Running the Course* section.

WRITER'S TOOLKIT 1: Bubble Chart

Essential for expanding the germ of an idea AND for taming a state of overwhelmed-by-ideas. To use frequently, and remind students to use it, as a good way to rev up for any exercise or writing project. See *Stimulus* section for details on this essential exercise, and **Mini-Lecture: Right Brain/Left Brain** for rationale.

WRITER'S TOOLKIT 2: Chaos Writing

Brilliant for breaking a block, and for letting off steam. See *Stimulus* section for how to run this exercise, and **Mini-Lecture: Right Brain/Left Brain** for rationale.

WRITER'S TOOLKIT 3: The Writer's Journal

Call it a writer's log, morning pages (Julia Cameron's term from The Artist's Way) or just a journal – this is urgent advice to your students to write to themselves about themselves. No exercise, I just wave my current journal at them (a hard-cover blank book is my choice, ideally with a colourful cover) and I give the reasons for keeping one:

- *It's completely private, completely yours, your space. Never 'show it off' or share it with anyone (though you can take bits out of it to use if you want).*

- *It is not a 'dear diary' or 'and then and then' record, not for practice writing of creative work; it is about you and your creative self (though some pieces of creative work may come through). It can be the place for your freewriting. You might describe the room or landscape or people around you, record and interpret your dreams, sound off about your family, job, creative work. You can vent grudges, doodle character sketches, be illogical and ungrammatical.*

- *Having said this, there are no rules, no shoulds! Do what you want with the space. But do try to write in it regularly.*

- *Patterns emerge. As you write, or when you read over, say 3 or 6 months of journal, you get an overview of what inspires you, motivates, what dispirits you, blocks you. The writing-for-no-reason gives you access to a subconscious fund of ideas, intuition, wholeness.*
- ***What's the point?*** *It feels good to know that someone (you) wants to know how you are doing on your writing path and in your whole life. The self-feedback gives you power, direction, energy.*

Some may ask about doing this writing onto their computer... it's a personal thing; I think pen in hand is more whole-self healing, and I like carrying my journal to work, to a coffee shop, on holidays for on-the-spot writing. Whatever works: that's the thing!

WRITER'S TOOLKIT 4: Focus Statement

This makes a nice tight 15 minute exercise that serves several purposes. Here's a sample tasksheet with definition and instructions.

Focus Statement

A declaration, 12 - 50 words (two to four lines), about the work you will write or are writing: what it is, its angle, point, purpose. Always put it in active present tense. It keeps you on track, may be the core of your query letter, of a pitch to an editor.

Example for a book:
Miss Quested's Return, a novel, is an exploration of Adela Quested, E M Forster's character from *A Passage to India.* In 1920s England following her disastrous trip to India, she embarks on new paths to solve the mystery of the caves, leading to discoveries about her personal, sexual and spiritual identity.

Instructions. *Write a focus statement for one of your own pieces of writing – or make one up!*

Read out. Have students read, even if work is rough, reassuring them that these little paragraphs can take several drafts and polishes to get right. **What's the point?**

- *The focus statement is a writer's tool to keep you on track. Stick a copy over your desk, your screen, on the cover of your notebook. Re-read it now and then as you research, as you write, if you get stuck in writing, when you self-edit.*
- *Some writers boil the statement down to just a sentence, a phrase or word. Gone with the Wind: determination.*
- *When submitting work, the focus statement is also the core of your query, proposal or coverletter.*
- *There you are at a party and you find you're standing next to an agent or editor – no umming and stumbling, the focus statement just trips off your tongue!*

WRITER'S TOOL KIT 5: Dealing with Procrastination

Adapted and excerpted from Writing on Both Sides of the Brain, by Henriette Anne Klauser, PhD, c 1986. Reprinted with kind permission of the author. www.henrietteklauser.com

Procrastination is a subject that is always greeted with laughs and groans – all writers seem to need help with it. I begin with an exercise, conclude it with a group pool of tips and intersperse a mini-lecture.

Stage 1. *Make a list of the ways you avoid writing.* (Allow 2-3 minutes; people don't have to finish this, it's just a starter.)

Stage 2. *Time's up. Now count your list. Who thinks theirs is the longest? Whoever's is longest is winner – and most creative!*

MINI-LECTURE 13: Procrastination

Adapted and excerpted from Writing on Both Sides of the Brain, by Henriette Anne Klauser, PhD, c 1986. Reprinted with kind permission of the author. www.henrietteklauser.com

Actually, congratulations to all. Procrastination is okay, it's part of the process of writing. It's natural, you're just being a writer! But what to do about it? Initially, two things.

- **Accept it.** *Procrastination is writing, incubating, pre-writing. Don't hate yourself. Learn to live with it and manage it; writers have to. My personal pattern is: When the pain of not writing gets worse than the pain of writing, then I write.*

- ***Use it.*** *Use the nervous energy to get things done. Can't settle, so you phone the dentist, write out the bill, fold the laundry... well, those things needed to be done, so at least give thanks for that! You can play one project off against another. But, if procrastination is getting the upper hand, there are ways...*
- ***Explore it.*** *Procrastination is resistance, says Henriette Anne Klauser in her book* Writing on Both Sides of the Brain. *We resist when we feel unsafe. Understand what's unsafe about the territory that you fear to tread, and you can choose, instead of being your own victim. Maybe you are...*
    - *Overinvested in being a writer, in writing this piece?*
    - *Overwhelmed by the work, amount of information?*
    - *Don't know where, how to start? This may include fear, but there are several possible fears, so you need to explore further. Is it...*
        + *Fear... of not being able to stop once started*
        + *Fear... of failure*
        + *Fear, strangely enough, of success. It goes like this: I'll finish this, and I'll sell it, and it will be a huge success and then Steven Spielburg will offer a film deal, and then I'll have to move to Hollywood, and then, oh gawd, Hollywood, all those swimming pools and face lifts, and what about the kids' school and I'll have to get the dog a passport and... and then I'll have to write another one!*
    - *Unwilling to commit? Choosing to write THIS means you shut out THAT – there is a real loss of other potentials (for now).*

All of this is rich material in getting to grips with your creative self, but procrastination can be insidious, paralyzing you with guilt and self-loathing. So, to remind yourself to explore, do as Klauser suggests in Writing on Both Sides of the Brain *and make a sign to put in your writing place, decorate it with colours and swirly letters:*
RESISTANCE ALWAYS HAS MEANING. [**Tutor:** hold up the sign you've made in advance!] *Your writing journal is the ideal place for exploring; some ways to set about it are:*

- **Analyse** the task, the tricks you have been using, how long you were procrastinating before becoming aware of it. A sort of report on yourself, to yourself, but not an attack, so you can see clearly instead of just suffering.
- **Chaos-write** about the task, how you feel about it, what's wrong with it so far, what's really worrying/distracting you. A cause or solution may pop out.
- **X-marks-the-spot** in the task, especially mid-project. If you freeze, go back to the work. Write in your journal: What was the last paragraph, the last sentence that I wrote? Where do I go from here? What happens when I finish this? Answers may reveal a flaw in intended direction of work, or fear you weren't aware of.
- **Bubble chart,** name of project in the centre – then everything that bugs you about it, all the reasons it's safer to not start or continue. Through this you may find a way to begin, organise, re-organise. Hidden obstacles may emerge, which you can then deal with directly.

PRACTICAL WAYS TO GET GOING

(Pool ideas with students, listing on board. Here are some for starters.)

1. Take just one small step. Divide work into bits.
2. Write anything – sheer drivel, chaos writing, middle of the piece, end
3. Write a letter to someone you know or a writer you admire (you don't have to send it)
4. Talk it through: What I really want to say is...
5. Timed treats – 15 min, 2 hours...
6. Trick yourself: 'Just 5 minutes...' plunge in
7. Tell yourself: writing is rewriting... this is just a draft I'll fix later

WRITER'S TOOL KIT 6: Dealing with the Critic Within

Adapted and excerpted from Writing on Both Sides of the Brain, by Henriette Anne Klauser, PhD. c 1986. Reprinted with kind permission of the author. www.henrietteklauser.com

Deep breath now, tutor, because this is a strange and psychological exercise that requires some bravery to conduct. I got it from Henriette Anne Klauser's book and embarked on it for myself, as she intended.

The effect was so extraordinary and useful that, after I'd been teaching for a while, I adapted it for class.

Do not do this immediately after **Dealing with Procrastination** as it treads on similar territory. I only ever run **Critic Within** about two-thirds of the way through a course, and I don't always do it – you need to judge that the class is ready and everyone feels mutually comfortable. You must do it yourself, alone at home and through all the phases, in order to understand it, believe in it and lead the class confidently.

A further caution: in any group of 12 students, one or two will just not GET this exercise, though most people find it does work. I've found this so reliably true that I now announce this fact, and reassure the class that if this happens, it's perfectly okay: not everything works for everyone.

Having warned you off, I must add that there are a lot of laughs from students during this mini-lecture and exercise, and you'll have fun delivering it with humour.

MINI-LECTURE 14: The Inner Critic

Adapted and excerpted from Writing on Both Sides of the Brain, by Henriette Anne Klauser, PhD, c 1986. Reprinted with kind permission of the author. www.henrietteklauser.com

The inner critic is the nagging faultfinder inside each of us. It uses sarcasm and name-calling: idiot, stupid, silly, arsehole; it makes us feel bad about our writing and trying to write. You also have a good critic within, a voice of reason which judges, chooses, edits and helps you WHEN YOU CALL ON IT. You can even have a helpful mentor within. The problem we all have is the sheerly negative critic within which erodes confidence, de-motivates, encourages procrastination. Henriette Anne Klauser, author of Writing on Both Sides of the Brain, says there are three phases to defusing your inner critic: get to know it, learn to talk back and engage in dialogue with it.

*1. **Get to know your critic***
Very often your critic is the internalisation of a real person past or present (a negative teacher, boss, partner, parent, sibling etc). For many people it isn't a real person, but an image that fits the internal negativity. You have to get to know how your critic sounds, behaves and looks, what tricks it uses to keep you from writing. Discovering its name and face puts you back in charge. If not a person, it might be a

mythological being, or something nonhuman, like a desert or a Dalek, or from film, like Oliver and Hardy, or the Wicked Witch of the West. Or a figure from art, a Jean Arp demonic sculpture, a Picasso abstract. Or a composite of several different critics.

You are going to ask your critic to come forward with an identity; it may come with its name, you might name it, or you might change its name. You recognise it by its voice or force – sneering, patronising, putting you down, dampening enthusiasm. Listen for limiting, cautionary words and attitudes: should, can't, ought, don't take risks, for your own good. This power expects giant leaps, instant success, dismisses positive steps you've taken. It will scoff at this exercise – that's its voice you'll feel, doubting and scorning.

Exercise begins:

RIGHT NOW, BECAUSE IT'S BEST NOT TO HAVE ANY PRECONCEIVED IDEAS ABOUT IT, I'D LIKE YOU TO MEET YOUR OWN CRITICS in the way Klauser sets out. We'll do this for just a few minutes, then at home you can do it for longer and develop it as I'll explain. You may dry up, resisting. Just say to the critic, 'That's okay, I guess there's nothing there, or nothing more.' But then ask, 'Is there anything else?'

So, put down your pens and paper, this is not a writing exercise. Sit quietly for a while, steady your breathing a bit, let go of tensions and thoughts, get peaceful. Close your eyes if you like.
    (silent time, about a half minute)
When you feel ready, invite your critic in cordially. You want to see what he looks like, hear the sound of her voice, notice what they have to say to you. You just want it to come forward and identify itself.
    (silent time, another half minute or minute)
When you have some kind of impression, ask it, Who are you?
    (silent time, a minute or several)
Okay, now thank your critic for coming out of hiding. Also, this is not supposed to be an exercise in schizophrenia, so say something to it like, let's get back together, or back underground you go – because of course the critic is you. And set a specific day and time when you will meet again, say next Wednesday at 9 or whenever. This is because, having

made the connection, you want to keep communication lines open.
    (another short silence)
Write about this, and any other meetings with your critic, in your writer's journal.

Tutor: when you are doing this for yourself at home, spend about 10 minutes on your first session of identifying your critic, and write in your journal afterwards. Also, a few days later, do the third stage for yourself (interview), but here and now in class, having sent students on this inner journey, the mood may be quite quiet; you may get some thoughtful feedback and the one or two students who say nothing happened (as you had warned). Your job now is to raise the mood, get them out of the trance-like state, by continuing with the mini-lecture.

Mini-Lecture continues

Adapted and excerpted from Writing on Both Sides of the Brain, by Henriette Anne Klauser, PhD, c 1986. Reprinted with kind permission of the author. www.henrietteklauser.com

2. Ways of dealing with your critic
Okay, now that you know your critic, what to do when it interferes with your writing? Talk back! As you get to know the critic you can learn to deflect it on the run, whenever it sneaks up on you. You can...

– Ask him politely to leave
– Tell her rudely to get out
– Talk about yourself in the third person, like a big protecting brother to yourself against the critic
– Say in your best American, 'Thank you for sharing that,' and move on, acknowledging but not arguing with the critic
– Mentally, visually, throw eggs at it, shrink it, decorate it with flowers, face paints, loo paper...

3. Other adventures with your critic: The Interview
Finally, there is a third stage of diminishing your critic's power – a dialogue. Conduct an interview in writing, both sides of it. As Klauser says in Writing on Both Sides of the Brain, this critic has been a dictator all your life, so act like you're a really tough journalist, pin this creep down. You want to uncover your critic's work habits and start being able to assert yourself.

Spend 20 minutes on this, in your journal. It might be easier to refer to yourself in the third person. Don't use yes-no questions, but ones to elicit specifics. One question may lead to another, deeper into an area – keep asking. Areas to cover:

- *The critic's identity – just how did you come into my life?*
- *What do you see as my problems in writing? What is it you don't like about my writing?*
- *What tricks do you use to persuade me?*
- *How do I get rid of you, get you to go away?*
- *What positive messages might you have for me?*

Now that last one may sound strange, but once you've wrestled with the critic for a while, he or she may, surprisingly, give you a grudging compliment or useful suggestion. Be warned! In the interview the critic may pull the 'for your own good' routine. You have to make him be honest, insist on your rights. And he hides things behind silence sometimes; go on to the next question.

Spend 20 minutes on a session and write it as you would an interview, pen to paper, question-answer, question-answer. As things heat up you may find that your handwriting comes out differently for each persona! It's best to think in terms of doing several sessions, developing an on-going relationship with your critic. Over time your critic can actually change and become quite manageable. Don't forget the end-session formalities as you return to this world: thank, send him away and schedule the next appointment.

WRITER'S TOOLKIT 7: Time and the Writer

This psychological mini-lecture might also be titled: More About Procrastination. Be sure to plan a completely unrelated quick writing exercise in the session, as this longish talk has little in the way of student participation. Also, in long-term planning, space out **Writer's Toolkits 5, 6 and 7,** or alternate years of using **6** and **7**, as **Time** is too heavy to run close to **Dealing With Procrastination** or **Critic Within.** I drew these ideas from a time management book by Sheila Dainow, The Time of Your Life, and adapted them to the writing life.

MINI-LECTURE 15: Your Right to Write

When you look closer at procrastination, at being stuck in your writing life or on a writing project, you'll find a definite cycle of successful delay. To do with how we tick inside, I sum it up as 'Why do I always shoot myself in the foot when I know I want to walk?'
Procrastination is resistance... resistance is reluctance to leave safety, to take risks. Now add to this a cycle of self-defeat: 'We know we SHOULD do something – we put it off so we feel GUILTY – we think about the effect of NOT DOING it so we feel ANXIOUS – so we know we SHOULD do it –' and so on. It can become such a struggle. Guilt, anxiety, depression, fear, worry give us a feeling of powerlessness. Powerlessness paralyses, so you stay stuck; you may even try to do something, but if it's ineffectual and you fail, you confirm your defeat – it's a downward spiral. There are four steps in understanding and combating the guilt-fear-defeat cycle. We'll start by giving not-writing a fair chance:

1. The rewards of not writing
Rewards for guilt: it is as if by feeling guilty you give yourself permission to continue with the behaviour – (Tutor, invite students to chime in with these, usually with laughs of recognition, including...)

- feeling bad is easier than doing the work of changing yourself
- if you feel guilty enough you'll be forgiven somehow for being naughty
- others take your professed guilt as caring about writing (but if you really did care you'd take action)
- guilt gets you sympathy
- guilt-fear-defeat stops you changing so you don't need to risk change
- you can blame others in your life for your guilty feelings, so you don't have to take responsibility

2. Finding time
Okay, let's put guilt and defeat aside for a bit and tackle one of the biggest moans writers make: I never have enough time to write! Well,

it takes determination but you CAN claw time for your writing life. All artists struggle to do it, and alas there is no magic recipe or gateway. One of the best ways to break the defeat cycle is to understand your own patterns.

First of all, start to be aware of your time thieves. Use your writer's journal to record them. There are cat burglars – little things that distract from what you have decided to do, like the telephone, like being too perfect at domestic or work chores, being 'nice' to the neighbour, the friend, the... whoever.

Then there are the big bullies, the mafia of thieves, which are patterns of belief about yourself and others, for instance, the mind-set that your family and your job must come before your writing. Seeing and combating these patterns takes insight – it's a process of growth, good to explore in your journal or to meditate on over time. Here are two insightful places to start: The Childhood Survival Guide and the Pyramid of Human Needs.

(**Tutor:** write or project these key points one by one on board)

Childhood Survival Guide
1. Must get it right
2. Got to please everyone
3. Must try hard
4. Got to be strong
5. Must do it fast

How familiar do these all feel! And our children feel it too! These early experiences still influence us and our attitudes to our use of time. They are deeply engrained habits and behaviour patterns, automatic reactions. They are very hard to fight off – and they aren't totally bad – but it would be good if they didn't control us. So, that's one area of awareness to dwell on. Developed by psychologist Claude Steiner, this is part of Transactional Analysis and its theories of what makes people tick. Two other TA pioneers – Abraham Maslow and Eric Berne – give me further fortification: we have a genuine right to write.

(**Tutor:** write the pyramid of needs on board or project from a prepared diagram)

PYRAMID OF HUMAN NEEDS
Abraham Maslow

**Creativity
&
fulfilling potential**

*Self-esteem; recognition;
feeling worthwhile & respected*

**Belonging; love;
acceptance; being part of a group**

Safety; protection from threat & danger

Basic body needs: food, water, shelter

Maslow and Berne have declared that these are all essential human needs. Of course the physical levels take priority, but if these are in place, the other needs are equally valid. They are all hungers, and if some categories are not being met life feels empty. You suffer.

Those psychological needs – self-esteem, recognition, creativity – are genuine. And they are your writing drive. So flap this pyramid in the face of anyone who dares try to stop you writing: INCLUDING YOURSELF! You have a genuine right to write, you are allowed to create… more than this, you must create and assuage that hunger, making your life meaningful to yourself.

PS – it can take some work over time to figure out what pushes your esteem-recognition buttons, who you are at your best, what your potential is, what your kind of creativity is. And you'll never have all those answers – but you will keep growing and creating!

3. Making time to write

Tutor, this takes a bit of nerve on your part, because you'll encounter mutterings of negativity. It forces students to encounter reality. Tell them: *You wish you had more time to write? The first step is to find your starting point. So let's do it right now in class.*

1) Get out your appointment diary, and look over your week for the next seven days. No diary? Sketch one out on a sheet of paper, leaving space for each day of the week, like a chart.

2) Look at your fixed times, think about the necessities of your week. Write them in – work hours, dropping and collecting kids, grocery shopping, dentist appointment...

3) Face reality – when can you write and for how long? Don't moan and groan! You feel or you see that it's impossible? You feel what's the use? Hey! That's the voice of patterns, or the critic within. Are you going to let it control you, defeat you? Start small; defuse the negativity. Somewhere there is a half-hour chunk of time, maybe two – or three! Or a half day, or two hours. Even if it is only one slot, write it in. Also, write in the task, a specific goal: 500 words; 2 pages; revise? Write one sentence?

4) Compare your week with your neighbour's (or small group work). Can you find any hidden time, times you hadn't thought of? During your daughter's ballet class? On the train commute?

5) If this is just too hard then you are gaining good insight into your patterns and your true priorities. Either accept them or work on changing them! Again, tracking yourself in your journal can help. So can the support of writing class and other writers.

That's it for the seven Writer's Toolkits. There are a few more wisdoms and exercises in this area which you might want to provide.

MINI-LECTURE 16: Right Brain/Left Brain

Tutor, make the chart of talents, or list as you talk, and conclude with a reading list handout (see **Sources**) and the physical waker-upper at the end of this mini-lecture.

Studies have lead to a theory that the two sides of the brain have different functions. In this split-brain theory of consciousness, the left side is logical, the right side creative. Many creative thinking specialists, including Buzan, Rico, Edwards, Klauser and others, have explored the subject: see the books on the handout to find out more. I like to think of it as the writer's dilemma.

Neither hemisphere is better than the other, but each has particular abilities – and in actuality they work together all over the brain, so this is just a model. The evolutionary advantage would seem to be that two modes of seeing and solving problems are better than one. In our waking state and Western world, the straight-thinking left is more in charge, and we need it, or we wouldn't be able to walk through a door, for instance. Dreams, gut-instinct, holistic perception – this is the domain of the right brain – and we need that for recognising faces and situations, for example. Dyslexia and autism may have something to do with split-brain misfunctions.

Left Brain talents	**Right Brain talents**
Speech/verbal • Logical	Spatial / Musical • Artistic
Linear • Detailed	Symbolic • Holistic / Gestalt
Sequential • Analytical	Simultaneous • Creative
Adult-like • Intellect, etc.	Child-like • Intuition, etc.
– active, quick, efficient (activates right side of body)	– receptive, wordless, timeless (activates left side of body)

So, you have the right brain's great seething, all-seeing, all-connecting stew of wordless wholeness – like dreams, like Chagall paintings. This is the creative source. And you have the orderly, organising, making-sense left side – logos, the word. This is the sorter and namer of things; it is also home of the censor, the critic within. The trick of writing, or any of the arts, is crossing, squeezing, sieving, dancing at the edge between the two modes.

Our earlier writer's tools – chaos writing and bubble charts – work because they get around the critical left brain. You write so fast and freely or jot in such bursts that the right brain freedom spills out, without the left brain interference. When rewriting you turn the logical mode loose to shape a piece of work with beginning, middle, end. Scientists have associated creativity with a state when both left and right brain are fully active and integrated.

It's interesting that the hemispheres cross-dominate physically, left brain activating the right side of the body, right brain the left. So, following a suggestion I read somewhere for an exercise to do before embarking on creative work, let's all stimulate our cross-lateral integration!

- *Stand up away from your table*
- *Raise your right knee and touch it with your left elbow (or hand, if elbow's too difficult). Lower it, then raise your left knee and touch it with your right elbow*
- *Go on, alternating, six times*

85 EXERCISE: A Happy Moan

Using established writers' wry warnings and personal experiences is a good way to liven up one of the *Process* lecture sessions, or to ready students for one of the deeper **Writer's Toolkit** exercises or just to stimulate supportive interaction. It's a pairing exercise, like **Quote-Match** in the *Stimulus* section. Back there I was suggesting it as a warm-up device; here the writers' quotes stir consideration of the writing life.

You can collect the quotes from your own readings of how-to books, the web, author interviews (see **Sources**), such as:

> Three hours a day will produce as much as a man ought to write. – Anthony Trollope

> The best time for planning a book is while you're doing the dishes. – Agatha Christie

Type quotes and cut up in strips (students can then take these away) or stick on cards (to hand back, saving you repeated sticky-fingerwork). Options:

- do in duplicates, distribute randomly and students have to find their match
- do as one-offs, students just turn to seat-neighbour to discuss both quotes
- do as one or two quotes per small group of 3-4 students
- you can leave out the author names, if you wish, to reveal at the end

Instructions: *Do you agree, disagree, find anything in common with the quote, with each others' experiences? Find 2-3 observations to report back on.* After the lovely chatter (5 minutes) the whole group pools comments – plenty of helpful tips and a mutual commiseration society! Usually I instigate the **Happy Moan** as an open-ended airing of writing griefs (procrastination and time always crop up); you can instead direct the subject by choosing quotes about beginnings, rejections, writer's block...

86 EXERCISE: Feel Free Joy

You need to be feeling good and confident with your class for this joy-of-creating activity because it's... different. An exhilarating demonstration of right brain access, it could preamble your **Right Brain/Left Brain Mini-Lecture,** or run any time you feel the course needs a fun, silly boost (with a message behind it). You'll need to spend some money, though once bought the materials will last for several years:

- Large pad of paper (A3, 11" x 16" or similar)
- 2-3 big sets of felt pens, a rainbow of colours
- 2-4 sets of crayons, many colours, variety of thicknesses
- 2 sets of coloured pencils
- a set of chalks or pastels...

In other words, go a bit wild when you buy (cheap and plentiful), looking for a range of textures as well as colours.

For the fun of it – and to signal that something different is afoot – arrange tables in small groups, if possible. Get everyone to put notebooks and clutter out of the way. We want acres of space. As you distribute a sheet of large paper to each student, tell them that we're going to have a free creative time. Then dump the many colouring tools in the middle of each table, pulling them out of their packaging – an effect of bounteous abundance, a cornucopia overflowing. Everyone is to take whatever colour calls, and start to fill the page – wild and free, whatever they feel like – abstract, so that perfectionism is banished. Change colours and textures at will, it's just colour and scribble and pattern for 5-10 minutes.

Usually there's an excited intake of breath, shy laughter, and then whole-hearted busy-ness and fond recollections of early school days. Interestingly, there are always joking comments about 'having them analysed' – people are self-conscious about being so free. I do my colour-scribbles along with the students, eventually saying how good it would be this free when writing... how one feels the urge, the instinct to a new colour, to a new shape... the wordless impulse of the creative right brain mode.

I also wander around and look and praise. Finally, to wind down, everyone holds up their page, or walks about appreciating the gallery, and we all feel gloriously free, giggly and creative.

Feel Free Joy variations.

- Use A-4 paper if preferred, especially if space is limited
- Do two rounds, the first spontaneous as above to warm up, the second: me and my writing. Each person can then talk about what the artwork represents as a way of talking about the writing life.
- Instead of colouring, make collages. Provide paste and lots of coloured paper and set students tearing, arranging, sticking.

II. INTO THE WRITING WORLD

Submitting work for publication and all that entails – market research, synopsis, approaches to agents, the realities of royalties and, of course, rejections – is part of living the writing life. As a working writer you have plenty of information on this process to impart. However, the majority of students are not ready for this stage, so I also encourage the entering of writing competitions. In the end, reading out in class, workshopping and contributing to a class anthology may provide all the audience that many students want. Nevertheless, forwarding the aim of ultimate publication widens writing horizons and keeps the ethos of the class serious (no matter how much fun you have).

> **MINI-LECTURE 17: Presentation, Presentation, Presentation**
>
> Unless you teach in very special circumstances, you should accept only typewritten work (except for in-class exercises). Writing this to you, a writer yourself teaching writing, I am not going to condescend to a detailed description of proper manuscript presentation. For years I told students the drill: *single side A4, double-spaced, indent paragraphs, Times New Roman, wide margins, pages numbered et cetera...* I backed this up with
>
> - examples of my own ms pages
> - insider explanation of why editors want it this way
> - confirmation that all the how-to books give details

... to little avail. Other tutors say the same: somehow students just don't hear you... or don't believe you... or can't be bothered? After a while I developed a detailed handout, including diagrams; I suggest you do the same.

Someone will ask: What about electronic submitting? There's a whole world of e-publication and e-zines out there, and no doubt special rules for these – check it out. However, in the ultimate print-world (the book has not died yet!), agents and editors generally want hard copy in conventional layout. If accepted, they'll ask for the ms on disc or by email.

MINI-LECTURE 18: Finding a Publisher or Agent

*Finding the **right** publisher or agent is what you really want, the one who will accept your work. An editor is not going to take on something unless she can sell it to her audience, no matter how wonderful the writing. There are directory listings in the writing 'bibles' (Writer's Handbook or Writers' and Artists' Yearbook) but to find acceptance you first must study your market.*

The method of sussing out a market applies to any medium – look for wordcount lengths, typical slots, general content and attitude: where does YOUR WORK fit? You wouldn't offer a gory forensic crime detection story to a women's domestic publication, you don't send lyrical prose pieces to a sci-fi publisher.

For books: from your own shelves, the library, Amazon.com and most of all, bookshops, look for books of a sort you'd like your own to be displayed with – what's your genre, category or author-type? Who publishes your kind of book? Read reviews, too, and note the publishers. You'll soon detect the difference between, say, a Black Swan book and a Fourth Estate book.

For popular short stories, study magazines carrying fiction, using two issues not more than one year old, so you can get a feel for the consistency of subjects, attitudes, tone. For literary short stories and poetry, study the 'little magazines' and competition anthologies (or websites) for the same reasons.

Agents do not handle short stories and poetry, there's not enough money in it. For books, they generally want to know that the book is finished (in case they love it, and they want it all NOW; and to know that you can finish a book). To shortlist agents, look for author acknowledgements and dedications in books similar to your own kind, to see if the author has thanked and named his/her agent.

To approach your chosen target, get names and addresses from the writers' 'bibles' and/or the internet. Often these state how they want to be approached. Do as they ask. Professionals are looking for professionalism.

Tutor, you can spend more time, even a mini-series, on introducing students to the publishing world. You could turn them loose on the writers' 'bibles', set an assignment to find three target markets, spend class time drafting approach letters. As a working writer you can talk about rejections, acceptances and money from personal experience. I always save this information til after the course's half-way mark. Be realistic, but avoid cynicism! Your job is to support, not shatter, your students. The crestfallen atmosphere as you gently dispel illusions of mega-deals is hard to take, so schedule an involving, upbeat writing exercise (see ***Stimulus*** section) or this entertaining **Titles** lesson to take the sting away.

87 EXERCISE: Titles

A good title really does help sell a book, both to editors and to the public. It also helps the writer, much as a Focus Statement does: to misquote Disney's genie in Aladdin, 'It's a whole great big novel (story/poem) packed into an itty-bitty space.' I liken titles to poetry; they are short, packed with meaning and resonance, and make good use of language and rhythm. Some people find titles easily, others say they need help, so here's a lively two-step exercise – and who knows, it might stimulate a few students into writing a piece to match the great title they devise.

Stage 1. *List three of your favourite or most memorable titles – books, films, plays, whatever comes to mind.* [Allow a few minutes.] *Okay, let's hear some.*

As you call on people there'll be oohs and ahs of recognition, triggers of other titles. Write them on the board, if you wish, and pretty soon begin to talk about **why** these are good and memorable.

MINI-LECTURE 19: What Should a Title Do?

*Why do our favourite titles work? They conjure emotions: an effective title **grabs** the reader, provoking or evoking an emotional response. It might intrigue, setting her dreaming (Gone with the Wind; other examples from the class's list). It might hint, tease, amuse or threaten, arousing the reader's interest (Don't Leave Me This Way). It may promise or sum up, conveying the essence of what follows (Pompeii). It may be spooky, sexy, horrifying, puzzling, solid, clever, fun, mysterious...* **Tutor:** again, draw on class contributions for examples as you list (and possibly hand out) the following.

Some Titling Guidelines

- Short is usually best (Cold Mountain); but very long sometimes works (The Curious Incident of the Dog in the Night-Time)
- It should be easy to say, easy to hear and understand. Though the exotic conjures well, be careful with foreign words which are difficult to pronounce and understand.
- Be aware of language: alliteration and rhythm help a lot
- Paradox and opposites appeal: Shadow of the Wind, Upstairs Downstairs
- Some sources
    Numbers – Benjamin Seven, Farenheit 451, Twelve Angry Men
    Alphabet – G is for Guilt
    Names – Jules et Jim, Oscar and Lucinda, Rebecca
    Place names – Watership Down
    Nursery rhymes, twisted clichés – Not a Penny More, Not a Penny Less
    Bible, hymns, Book of Common Prayer
    Shakespeare, Milton, other poets
    Standard successful titles – The Truth About..., Behind the Scenes at...

Exercise continues.

Stage 2. Prepare in advance photocopies of pages of the Bible, Shakespeare sonnets, Milton. Cut into half or quarter-page chunks, as a whole page of one of these rich sources is overwhelmingly full of title possibilities.

Instructions. Distribute a different source sheet to each student.

Right, so here's the Bible, Shakespeare and Milton – have a go and raid them for ripping good titles, do a list. Not for your own work in hand (though that's okay if you find one), but just anything that feels and sounds like a good title. You can twist or adapt words and phrases as you like.

Allow a good 5-10 minutes, then **read out** – it's great fun. You and the class can also hazard guesses as to what kind of story it will be, which leads nicely into talking about genres and tone – how you can tell something is a crime story v a romance.

MINI-LECTURE 20: Other Avenues for Publication

Besides the mainstream there are several smaller worthwhile pathways to publication you should encourage students to take. (See *Sources* for listings)

Competitions. The Bridport, Wells, Asham, Fish, World Wide Writers, London Writers, Phillip Good… these are annual fixtures with good judges, good prizes and good quality winners. There are many more around, and checking their websites or sending for their leaflets and anthologies is the only way a student can judge the parameters. As well as prize money, some promise publication, some make links with mainstream editors/agents – all good stuff. Tell students they MUST study the requirements and follow the rules – heed wordcount, use presentation conventions. This is excellent 'realities of writing' training, and the deadlines are goads. I bring in comps brochures to share, and so do students, and I do a termly handout listing key details of the main competitions, titling it **Set Your Goals.**

Not winning is akin to the rejection experience, so that's a reality, too. Explain how a writer has to nurture himself/herself through the hurt, send off work to the next competition, and recover into writing new work. Assure students that even being short-listed is a kudo. Point out competitions which offer critique services, so at least something is gained, even if nothing is won.

Little magazines. Little because the circulation is small (usually with a devoted subscribership), the pay zilch, but the quality of the fiction and poetry is often high, and not of the commercial, mainstream sort.

Often respected by mainstream editors/agents. Bring a couple of these to class, like Ambit and QWF, but insist students send for and read an issue or two before submitting; each title has its own flavour, so market research is essential and students must evaluate publications against their own standards.

Websites. A whole wonderful world of writing and cyber-publication. I'm a print person myself, but the web is with us, so suggest students explore this market.

Self-Publication. This used to be anathema to any self-respecting writer, but with the aggrandizement of the publishing industry some authors are justified in self-publishing. If the target market is precise and small, say a regional guide, recipes or memoire it may be worth doing, and like those dream-about-it megabucks book deals maybe it'll take off and get picked up by a mainstream publisher; novels, unlikely. Warn students off vanity presses which ask the author for heaps of money. Ensure they know they must do their own sales, marketing and distribution.

TIP: Writer's Support
Let your fledglings fly and inform them about sources of support out there in the world beyond class. See *Sources* for some listings.

---

88 EXERCISE/ACTIVITY: Celebrate! Class Anthology

A group project to publish a collection of class members' work has plenty of learning in the process and makes a wonderful souvenir of a productive, creative time together. Bring in previous class anthologies, unfancy literary magazines or competition anthologies and propose the idea 4-6 weeks before the end of the course. Distribute them for study and then lead the class to decisions on:

Class Anthology

- Contents (theme? free choice of submissions? something done during the course? something new?)
- Title

- Format and quantity perhaps your institution will produce a photocopied booklet (after all, it is evidence of student achievement), perhaps you and the students will have to club together to pay for reproduction. It can be as simple as A4 pages stapled down the side. Discourage anything too ambitious for the sake of expenses and time (they should be creating their writing, not agonizing over typefaces!).
- Space allowance per student (there may not be room for a complete short story each)
- Layout; clearly defined ms submission guides
- Deadline

Tutor, don't take it all on yourself: assign students to assemble, collate, type contents, write forward, self-written author blurbs. You're not being lazy, you are giving students a lesson in the editor's and publisher's role. Aim for distribution in the final class to end the course with a flourish.

Section 5

RUNNING THE COURSE: Enriching elements

I. Workshopping

II. Using a Class Text

III. Managing Discussions

IV. Sensitive Flowers & Other Pitfalls

V. Feedback, Tutorials & Assignments (or Not)

Section 5

RUNNING THE COURSE: Enriching Elements

There can be even more to a strong, supportive writing class than exercises, information and the nurturing environment. This section suggests methods I've discovered for workshopping, discussions, text analysis and assignments. A bonus – these draw on the students' own energy, making tutor a ringmaster instead of having to be the sole provider of all content. Furthermore, as well as benefiting students, these elements support the tutor by bringing an underlying organisation and drive to the course. Also here: teaching pitfalls and tutor backup.

I. WORKSHOPPING

Naturally you'll have students reading out their exercises done in class – it provides a glow of pride, instant feedback and good learning material for all. Consider as well the grown up version of reading out: workshopping.

Beginners to creative writing won't be ready for this, and even those who are more experienced may be unwilling to commit early in a term, but writers who really want to progress want to workshop their writing. As a writer yourself I presume you know that this means reading out to the class their own home crafted piece of writing (whether it began as a class exercise or is entirely their own). Peers and tutor then constructively comment on the piece, so the author can judge what works and what needs improving. It is good learning material for the whole class, not just the author.

Some tutors and writing circles run workshops very loosely, just seeing who wants to read on the day. In my experience it's far better to get writers to book scheduled slots, for two very important reasons. First, tutor organisation. You need to know if you will have readers and how many, so you know how to plan class content. Using the ad hoc method could leave you with too many readers (your plans wasted) or too few (vamping to fill class time).

The second main advantage: scheduled workshopping works

hugely to the students' benefit. Getting your writers to commit to reading out on a certain date provides a deadline – we all hate 'em, but they make us write! Assignments, 'homework', our opus in progress… these can be fudged, but a performance, not. Students report time and again in end-of-course feedback that workshopping really helps. Scheduling also ensures fair turns, rather than the same extraverts monopolising class time.

Setting up for workshopping. In the first class, or when you deem your class ready, explain the idea and circulate a sign-up sheet: an example, which also explains how the workshopping runs, given below. Allow two weeks to collect commitments, then take the draft away, type in the names and distribute photocopies. Coloured paper makes it easier for students to keep. Each week verify that your following week's readers are on target; always have a back-up exercise (or a chunk of your own writing) stowed away in case of sudden no-shows.

Workshopping: Schedule for reading/feedback
Term 1: Autumn 2010 Wednesdays. 7:00 - 9:30 pm, Room 41

- Two writers get group feedback per session, half an hour maximum per person; break at 8pm; exercises or discussion from 7:00 pm.
- As a guide, 2100 words takes about 15 minutes to read, and allows 15 minutes for discussion; this is about 5 - 6 pages double-spaced. (Time it yourself at home). Less is fine. Talk to me if in doubt.
- GIVE TUTOR A COPY to read along with you, and TO KEEP for course records. You may also provide copies for the class to have sight of as you read.
- This DOES NOT eliminate unscheduled readouts or readings of short exercise pieces! We still have time for those on an ad hoc basis.
- IF YOU HAVE TO MISS A SCHEDULED SLOT, please arrange a swap with another writer in the class; if this is not possible, please advise tutor.

Readings:		8:30	9:00
Week 3) 1/10	exercise	John Edwards	Marie Archer
Week 4) 8/10		Gilbert James	Rosalind Kaczyk

… et cetera, numbering and dating each class to the end of the term; be sure students enter commitments in their own diaries too! Except for text discussion dates (see later) I prefer to be non-committal about scheduling other class content, to allow flexibility.

Workshopping Tips

- Schedule shown is for a 2½ hour class – ideal for workshopping. You can manage three workshops in that time, if you and your class wish, allowing only a half-hour or so for tutor content input. You can fit one or two workshops in a 2 hour class, again depending on class needs.

- I like to run the two workshops back to back, a precise 30 minutes each, after class content (exercises, discussion or mini-lecture). This way we do our lively work first, then settle to listen and concentrate.

- Before embarking on workshopping, see **Writing and Reading Out** in *Nurture* section and **Managing Critique,** below, to combine into a mini-lecture and guidelines.

- It's helpful if author distributes ms copies, perhaps only one-between-two class members, so the work can be seen as well as heard. Someone always suggests we distribute copies the week prior, and I've encouraged this... but student commitment doesn't stretch this far in reality.

- Tutor is timekeeper: be firm and fair about starting and ending each workshop on time. If someone reads for too long he/she must get less feedback time.

- I put the reader-out at the tutor's desk and move to sit in his or her place. Three reasons: best sight and sound lines for the class; good practice for the author in presentation skills; tutor becomes a peer among equals, not the sole voice of approval.

- Inspired by workshopping styles of a master's degree in creative writing, I now use the 'fly-on-the-wall' method. I remind the author, when finished reading, that she/he must just watch and listen as peers discuss the work. I regularly have to remind the peers, too. This takes a while to get used to, and tutor has to crack the whip sometimes, but it's much more constructive and efficient than allowing the author to explain or defend. Invite the author to rebut or explain in the last few minutes of the session.

- As well as verbal critique, I instituted 'little notes' for feedback thanks to an idea from a class member (Hi, Mel!). Save 3-5 minutes before the end of the half hour slot (as author rebuts), so students can write a brief message to the author – it may be a note of encouragement, a contradiction of a critical comment, or a small praise or crit not raised verbally. This way everyone gets to 'speak out'; authors greatly enjoy reading these at home, and benefit from the extra input.

- Remind all the class, as well as author, to jot notes, so that comments will be specific. This develops all students' critical abilities.

Managing class critique. The tutor's role is to 'conduct' the criticism and set the tone and guidelines. Formal workshopping is not identical to exercise read-rounds, so see **Suggestions on Reading Out, Commenting and Receiving Criticism** in *Nurture* section and top up with the workshopping specifics below. Deliver as a mini-lecture and handout. Because this is writing of some length honed at home, some students may be extra sensitive to critique.

WORKSHOPPING GUIDELINES

You as the Reader:

(1-2 as Section 1 Nurture guidelines)

3. On the other hand, do say 'This is a short story,' or 'This is about half-way through my novel.' Also, it's a good idea to direct the criticism before you read by stating a specific worry. 'I'm afraid I'm giving away too much at the start.' 'I need a good title for it.' 'Does the dialogue work.'

You as a Critiquer:

(1-6 as Section 1 Nurture guidelines)

7. Don't question the author directly: my classes use the 'fly-on-the-wall' method. The author only watches and listens as peers discuss the work.

8. My classes follow the workshop with a 'little note', a few minutes to jot comments direct to the author. This is also the place to indicate small punctuation errors, typos or misspellings, or mark them on the ms if one is provided. Please give your name so author can further discuss with you if desired.

You, Reading and Receiving Criticism

1. Just listen and absorb. You are a 'fly-on-the-wall', not rising to each point or question. It's extremely useful to hear others debate their responses to your work. Write down what people say, ideally on the ms, even if you don't agree.

(2-3, as Section 1 Nurture guidelines)

II. USING A CLASS TEXT

To my knowledge having a book which the class reads in common is not normally done in standard adult education prose creative writing classes or writers' circles. Those in the serious institutional business of growing writers – universities and A-level English courses – include analysis of published works. Along with workshopping, I've adopted a class text as a backbone for my courses. For one thing, astonishingly, some wannabe writers do not read – this must be corrected immediately! Generally, though, most writing students love talking about books but take heed, you do not want to drift into a lit-crit course. Structured discussion (see below) once a month or once a term is about right; as well as this it's extremely useful to be able to refer to a work in common to illustrate a craft point. Think of the characterisation of Vermeer's wife in Tracy Chevalier's Girl with a Pearl Earring, the cliffhangers in Dan Brown's The Da Vinci Code, Mark Haddon's use of language in The Curious Incident of the Dog in the Night-Time.

What to choose? Preamble with a mini-lecture to float the idea and steer the class toward a consensus, or give a shortlist and some guidance. A genre novel, a best-seller, a literary prize-winner – all good possibilities. Paperbacks, of course, for affordability. Or you can impose a choice. For years I have used New Writing, annually published under the aegis of the British Council, an anthology that very usefully contains short stories, novel extracts, poems and non-fiction, all by current and rising new writers. I've yet to find another anthology that does this.

MINI-LECTURE 21: Reading for Writers

To improve writing craft it helps to look at how other writers – in their various ways – create mood, develop characters, weave a narrative, use language. Novel, short story, memoir, biography, drama, feature article all have narrative in common. Many poems do, too. Fiction is our chief focus, but across all disciplines the devices are similar for capturing audience attention, holding it, and unrolling what a writer has to say. We are looking at writers as writers ourselves.

Tutor preparation. If an anthology, tutor has to read through and select which pieces will be discussed – my students requested a list as a handout, so they could read in advance: makes intensive summer reading for me! Issue an anthology list at first or second session. For a book, wait til the class is gelled before making the group choice. I do one book per term plus about 12 paired pieces from the anthology over a year.

Set the discussion date(s) only when term is underway in order to maintain flexibility for other course content. Anthology or book, you've got to analyse the chosen works yourself, even if loosely. Remind students weekly to read for the upcoming discussion date.

III. MANAGING DISCUSSIONS

I used to be afraid of discussion, worried that it would be directionless, take over the class and possibly lead to arguments – but the experience of conducting workshopping gave me confidence, and the introduction of **Reading for Writers** helped me figure out a method. It has two key elements: a directive to **focus** discussion, and **pair-work** to give everyone a chance to be heard. First, the **discussion guide,** to give as a handout with mini-lecture at the first discussion session; print it on coloured paper to help students keep it throughout the course.

Reading for Writers Discussion Guide

STRUCTURAL ELEMENTS – What is the backbone of the work at hand?
Identify beginning, turning points, climax, end, themes.

CHARACTERS – Are characters and characterisation believable?
What is the chief question of the protagonist? His/her chief conflict/obstacles.

NARRATIVE COMPONENTS – How is the story told, what tells it?
What use of devices such as point of view, show v tell, dialogue, action, flashback, monologue, letters, settings, symbols etc

VOICE, PACE & GENRE – What is the author's style (bouncy, dark, lyrical...)?
How does the language contribute to voice? Is the pace fast, leisurely, varied? How is pace achieved, to what effect? Would this author's work be appropriate or not to different genres such as crime, mainstream, literary, women's magazine fiction, and why?

CRAFTY – What tricks and devices, methods and techniques can we (you) borrow or adapt from this writer?

The paired discussion. After distributing the discussion guide, walk round the room and assign neighbouring students ONE of the topics from the sheet to focus on as a pair. To students say: *Obviously, you'll stray into other areas, because writing is organic, but try to stick to this point, and after ten minutes we will all come back together and pool our observations. Remember, we are looking at this piece as writers, to help our own writing.*

Then off they go, chattering away. Listen in casually from pair-to-pair; add good points you overhear to the whole-group work at the end. Tutor is timekeeper, giving a two-minute warning, so each pair will have gathered some points to contribute to the whole. If you don't assign all the topics it still works, or you can assign the same topics to more than one pair, or you can put two topics together. You'll inevitably get students who have not read the work (grrrrr!); have a non-reader join a reading pair to listen in. Even one topic could fill up a whole session of discussion, and analysing can go on for ages (but we don't want a lit-crit course, we want to write, right?), so tutor will have to close the chatter and open up the pooled commentary, calling on each pair and encouraging other comments. Use the whiteboard to focus notes on each of the discussion points: what works, what doesn't? – pros, cons, compare-contrast if you've used two pieces.

Draw on your preparatory analysis to augment student observations and conclusions if anything important has been missed, rather than a straight lecture.

Discussion planning options. Structuring discussion of published work into a session is flexible. Depending on your other agendas for the course, it can

- stand alone in the session – altogether it'll take a minimum 30 minutes, or could fill a whole half session before or after break
- lead to mini-lecture or other work on marketing, point of view, characterisation or any other topic you make relevant
- be springboard for a writing exercise – modelling an opening, a setting or dialogue scene, for example; or taking a character or situation and veering off in another direction; changing p.o.v or tense et cetera – see *Craft* and *Stimulus* sections

- the same method of giving pairs a focussed discussion task is a good way to get students exploring any subject you wish to cover

> **TIP: Student contribution** once or twice over a course is a great way to give yourself a break from the burden of finding teaching material. Ask everyone to bring in their **favourite opening** of a novel, for instance, and you have the makings of an excellent discussion. Of course some will forget, so bring some spares for these people.

IV. SENSITIVE FLOWERS & OTHER PITFALLS

A small warning here. Teaching writing is a bit of a loaded situation for the tutor, because part of the student agenda is 'make the magic happen for me'.

- Creative writing often attracts a few people who've had a bumpy mental or emotional ride. The experience may be their subject, or may colour their writing; unless you are trained in counselling and running a writing-as-therapy class, don't go too deep in helping or criticising.
- See **Tutor Ground Rules & Support** in Section 1, *Nurture*.
- You may encounter the blocked student whose internal negativity comes out as disguised hostility toward tutor and peers. These students often present old work, may do only one new piece in a whole year. They usually have excellent critical abilities. If you get a really negative person, take him or her aside and chat, point out their power, its effect on others.
- Another form of resistance is the student who always wants to know 'why are we doing this exercise?' or 'what good is this?' Remember, it's not really that they don't trust you... they're just a wee bit afraid inside. Regard them as useful gadflies.
- Each class has its own energy. If somehow one leaves you feeling a bit low, don't blame it on yourself, especially if you know you

have other classes that work well. Could be you have a majority of introvert personalities – don't worry, they are getting plenty from you, they just don't have the need to give back like extraverts do.

- If you feel really undermined, don't cave in under negativity. Consult an experienced fellow tutor and/or call for support from your team leader or another manager.

- Then you have the opposite challenge, a fan club of repeat-repeat students. This puts a burden on you, the pressure to come up with more new exercises (may this book help you!). **Reading for Writers** and **Workshopping** provides fresh material each year, and of course these committed students will be writing new stuff – so just take it as a compliment!

V. FEEDBACK, TUTORIALS & ASSIGNMENTS (OR NOT)

Besides instant responses when reading out exercises and workshopping how does a student know how she/he is doing? And how to do better? Feedback from the tutor.

Feedback on the page. However you structure the receipt of student writing (see below), you should return it with comments to the author written on the page – ticks or small queries in the margin, several summary sentences of response (praise as well as criticism) on final page. I've known tutors who type a paragraph of feedback – gluttons for punishment, I say!

I like to put a positive phrase on the first page too *(Great title!* or *good opening* or similar) – we all need encouragement. Couch criticism carefully, but DO criticise – writers need to know what's not working. It's a joy when students rework a piece incorporating tutor and peer feedback: they really are learning to write better.

Tutorials. I feel that a one-to-one session of 10 minutes at least once in a course is the ultimate in tutor feedback. The subject can be a specially submitted piece of writing, or just a 'how my writing is going' personal chat. You can explain a problem and suggest solutions much more specifically than in comment on the page.

Tutorials are fun but they take organisation. Don't do them outside your paid hours! I schedule them as I do workshopping – sign-up sheet and diaries in hand. Allow 2-3 ten-minute slots per session over several weeks, taking a half-hour from the start or end of normal class. The one-to-one involvement is too draining for a tutor see all students in one long session. You can't cheat the others while you see the few, however, so leave a stimulus exercise for the rest of the class (like **Sweetie Jar** or **I remember**…). You have to organise your rooming, too – I use the normal classroom for tutorial, let the others scatter in canteen or public areas. Be a strict timekeeper, or other tutees and your own energy will be messed up.

Assignments (or not). So, can creative writing be taught? Can you make people write, and write better? Your students joined because they want to write, but some just won't, they'll simply coast along feeling like writers. A few are genuinely and steadily writing. Others write when they have a deadline, they WANT a deadline. Scheduled workshopping serves this purpose; assignments do too. Not everyone will comply, but aim for two assignment deadlines per term as realistic for adult part-time courses.

And, dear tutor, there's another reason to harvest assignments. Adult education institutions these days usually require evidence of course planning, aims and outcomes.

Obstacle: creative writing as homework?? Pleasing teacher is exactly what creativity should NOT be. Here's my multi-level scheme to encourage maximum freedom under the banner of assignment. First, devise an assignment, usually springboarding from class work. For a beginners' general course you'll work through a range of disciplines and ask for examples from each student. In creative prose courses, base assignments on the topics in *Craft*. Set the deadline and – supported by an explanatory handout – instruct students to interpret the assignment in one of three ways. The objective is to go with the flow – but whatever the flow, students produce writing. Anyone may be at an Alpha or Beta phase, even published writers.

> **Creative Writing Assignment Scheme**
>
> **Alpha** – you are looking for ideas, stuck, open to new avenues, groping around, exploring, want some fun. Do the set assignment.
>
> **Beta** – you have the germ of an idea or bits and pieces, want to expand or need different angles. Use your own ideas (characters, situation, story etc) within the assignment.
>
> **Delta** – you are deeply engaged in a particular work. Do not let assignments distract you. Instead, write and hand in another scene, chapter, etc

Feedback v grades: I'm extremely uncomfortable with any grading on creative writing – how would you, as a writer, like to get a rejection with a numerical ranking on it? But if officialdom needs a performance indicator (NEVER on students' work, only in tutor records), I note 1 *for excellent/very good/hardly any weaknesses*, 2 *for good, some weaknesses, satisfactory,* 3 *for some competence, but many weaknesses*, 4 *for weak, but made an effort,* 0 *for made no effort.* The student only sees my feedback comments on the ms, as described above. To me, if students are trying to write, if they are producing writing, they're learning and growing to their own measure – that's what counts in creative development.

Feedback questionnaire. Having made writing class all fun and games you'd think a questionnaire would be sneered at by students, but introduced persuasively they happily buckle down to a bit of form-filling. Done both midway and at the end of every course, students gain useful self-reflection AND give you evidence of learning. Do a shorter version even for a one-day course. The comments are your tutor 'report card' to help you improve your course next time. We had the **Start of Year Questionnaire** in *Nurture,* here's an **end of year** example; in your own version leave space to write under each question – you don't want an essay, just a few sentences of thoughtful response.

> **END OF COURSE QUESTIONNAIRE: A SUMMING UP**
>
> 1. Identify one or two points of feedback on your work in workshopping. Say how you feel about the criticism. Describe if or how you made use of the feedback in your work.
>
> 2. Identify points gained from hearing others' work read out. Why or how was it useful to you?
>
> 3. Describe any ways the class helped your organization of yourself as a writer, e.g. write regularly, prepare manuscripts to professional conventions, meet deadlines, research markets, research content, submit work...
>
> 4. What is your favourite piece from the *New Writing 12* anthology – and why? (See the anthology or anthology reading list to remind yourself.)
>
> 5. Exercises included: *Bubbling, Character Profile, Monologues, Characterisation from a word, Agony Letter, Rainbow Tales, 8 Senses, Dialogue from given line, Titles, Dream...* which of these were most useful to you, and why?

Tutor: Some self-reflection for you, too! It's a good idea, after every class as you put your teaching stuff away, to stop a moment and note on the back of the class plan things that fell flat, things that went well, so you can tweak improvements and develop your successes.

So here we are, at the end of our course. Be organic and instinctive in using this book, devise, adapt, invent. Teaching itself is creative, have a good year, have fun! You'll find it true that the teacher learns from students – have a good writing year yourself.

SOURCES and bibliography (In alphabetical order within sections)

Section 1: Nurture
Rogers, Jennifer, *Adults Learning,* Fourth Edition, Open University Press, Buckingham, 2001 (and earlier). A classic of practical insights and methods for teaching adults.
Browsing materials: see Writer's Support Sources, below.

Section 2: Stimulus
Brande, Dorothea, *Becoming a Writer,* Papermac, London, 1983. Orginally published in 1934 and still valid, inspiring and helpful today.
Buzan, Tony, *The Mind Map Book,* BBC Books, London, 1995.
Clanchy, Kate, poet and tutor. See the British Council site www.contemporarywriters.com
Goldberg, Natalie, *Writing Down the Bones,* Shambhala, Boston, 1986. A classic of inspiration by now, and a joyful discovery for anyone new to writing.
Klauser, Henriette Anne, *Writing on Both Sides of the Brain,* HarperCollins, New York, 1986. Really useful insights and techniques on the writing process. Also see her *Write it Down, Make it Happen,* Simon & Schuster, London, 2001. See www.henrietteklauser.com
Metzger, Deena, *Writing for Your Life,* HarperSanFrancisco, New York, 1992.
Rico, Gabriele Lusser, *Writing the Natural Way,* Tarcher/Putnam, GP Putnam's Sons, New York, 1983. Vignettes, clusters, right-brain and lots more.
Roberts, Michele, *During Mother's Absence,* Virago, London, 1994. Une Glossaire/A Glossary and short stories, too. See the British Council site www.contemporarywriters.com
Rekulak, Jason, *The Writer's Block,* Running Press, Philadelphia, 2001. 786 ideas to jump-start your imagination.

Section 3: Craft
Allnutt, Gillian, poet. See the British Council site www.contemporarywriters.com
BBC *Get Writing* website, www.bbc.co.uk/dna/getwriting/ A great source.
Binchy, Maeve, *The Lilac Bus,* Arrow, London, 1987. The scene suggested is on pp 22-23.
Burroway, Janet, *Writing Fiction:A Guide to Narrative Craft,* Fourth Edition, HarperCollins College, New York, 1996. A deeply considered and practical university fiction-writing textbook.
Ensign, Georgianne, *Great Beginnings,* HarperCollins, New York, 1993. Extracted openings from scores of novels, organised by method.
Goldberg, Natalie, *Writing Down the Bones,* as above. The Vivid Verbs exercise is adapted from 'Action of a Sentence', p 87.
Kerr, Katherine, daughter, cinquain-writer and psychologist.
Knight, Damon, *Creating Short Fiction,* Third Edition, St Martin's Griffin, New York, 1997. Author of over 80 short stories, 14 novels and more, he also writes a solid how-to-write.
Lukeman, Noah, *The Plot Thickens,* Robert Hale, London 2002. Good focus, with exercises, on the character-driven story.
Novakovich, Josip, *Fiction Writer's Workshop,* Story Press Books, Betterway Books, F+W Publications, Cincinnati, 1998. Sound, no-nonsense, plenty of exercises.
Ray, Robert J, *The Weekend Novelist,* Dell, New York, 1994. Inspiring AND practical, a great help in getting to grips with writing fiction, especially structure and character. An update is *The Weekend Novelist* by Ray and Bret Norris, A&C Black, London, 2005.
Sellers, Susan, ed, *Taking Reality by Surprise,* The Women's Press, London, 1991. Coloured Runes exercise, p 55, by Joan Downar. Collective Dialogues exercise, p 35, by Gillian Allnutt. This creative, supportive book is chock full of exercises.
Seuling, Barbara, *How to Write a Children's Book and Get It Published,* Scribner's, New York, 1991. Good advice for all writers.
Trapido, Barbara, novelist and tutor. See the British Council site www.contemporarywriters.com
Turner, Sylvia, *Rhyme and Reason,* Collins Educational, 1996. Poetry forms explained, crystal clear and fun because it's for children.
Ur, Penny and Wright, Andrew, *Five-minute Activities: A Resource Book of Short Activities,* Cambridge University Press, Cambridge, 1992. Descriptive Powers exercise is adapted from 'My neighbor's cat', p 54 Brilliant for language teachers, some ideas adaptable for creative writing.

Section 4: Process
Brande, Dorothea, *Becoming a Writer*, as above.
Cameron, Julia, *The Artist's Way* and *Vein of Gold*, Pan, London, 1995 and 1997. Inspiration, practical help and great comfort in finding one's creative self. I recommend her to all.
Dainow, Sheila, *The Time of Your Life*, Boxtree, London, 1994. About managing your life and demands.
Galin, David, MD, *The Two Modes of Consciousness and the Two Halves of the Brain*, *Symposium on Consciousness*, American Association for the Advancement of Science, Viking Press, NY, 1974. Scientific brain-mind discussions.
Goldberg, Elkhonon, *The Wisdom Paradox: How Your Mind Can Grow Stronger as Your Brain Grows Older*, Gotham, New York 2005.
Goldberg, Natalie, *Writing Down the Bones*, as above.
Kerr, Michael, partner and author.
Klauser, Henriette Anne, *Writing on Both Sides of the Brain*, as above.
Rico, Gabriele Lusser, *Writing the Natural Way*, as above.
Winokur, Jon, *Writers on Writing*, Running Press, Philadelphia, 1990. Hundreds of quotes about the many processes of writing from hundreds of well-known authors.
Writer's 'bibles' and Competitions: see Writer's Support Sources.

Section 5: Running the Course
Anthology: *New Writing*, editors change each year, published annually in association with the British Council, see www.britishcouncil.org/arts-literature
Murray, Donald M, *A Writer Teaches Writing*, 2nd Ed, Houghton Mifflin, Boston, 1985. For American university composition teachers, insights and practical ideas for all writing tutors.

Writer's Support Sources (Just for starters...)

Books: All of the books listed under **Stimulus**, **Craft** and **Process** above, plus the writer's 'bibles': *The Writer's Handbook*, ed Barry Turner, Macmillan, London, annually; and/or *Writers' and Artists' Yearbook*, A & C Black, London, annually. Useful articles change every year, and market listings, of course, are essential.

Magazines: Regular encouragement through the letterbox, and, tutor, these are good sources for exercise ideas. *Mslexia*: Quarterly aimed at women; the tone is professional and supportive; men can benefit too. www.mslexia.co.uk *Writers' News* (newsy) also publishes *Writing Magazine* (how-to-write-y), both monthlies. Encouraging but smack of the amateur sometimes. www.writersnews.co.uk *Writer's Digest*: Monthly American, but fatter than two UK mags together and full of a wide range of advice. www.writersdigest.com

Websites: As well as www.bbc.co.uk/dna/getwriting the sites of the magazines listed above are extremely helpful, and try www.qwfmagazine.co.uk .There are heaps of others. Try publishers' and agents' sites, too, like www.bloomsbury.com

Competitions and 'little magazines': Contact national and local Arts Councils, and see the writers' 'bibles', magazines and websites above for current listings.

Courses, local or residential, and author talks: For students wanting variety, tutors wanting work, everyone wanting inspiration: contact local boroughs, ask at libraries, search the net for adult education centres, arts centres and book events. The best-known residential workshop is the Arvon Foundation, which provides a week in the deep country with two tutors and about 16 participants. Others well established: Ty Nwydd in Wales and Indian King Arts Centre in Cornwall. Find these through the web or writers' bibles. Haye-on-Wye, Oxford and Chichester are among annual festival fixtures with dozens of authors reading, talking, signing.

Organisations: Collaborative trade bodies for professionals, but kind to the as-yet-unpublished: *Society of Authors* and *Writers' Guild of Great Britain*. The former is long-established, the latter has a stronger broadcast emphasis; both cover all writing areas. www.societyofauthors.net and http://cgi.writersguild.force9.co.uk Look for writers' circles and local networking groups, too. In London: Women Writers Network, www.womenwriters.org.uk